ROUTLEDGE LIBRARY EDITIONS:
LIBRARY AND INFORMATION SCIENCE

Volume 96

TECHNOLOGY TRANSFER

T0384468

TECHNOLOGY TRANSFER
The Role of the Sci-Tech Librarian

Edited by
CYNTHIA STEINKE

Routledge
Taylor & Francis Group
LONDON AND NEW YORK

First published in 1991 by The Haworth Press, Inc.

This edition first published in 2020
by Routledge
2 Park Square, Milton Park, Abingdon, Oxon OX14 4RN

and by Routledge
52 Vanderbilt Avenue, New York, NY 10017

Routledge is an imprint of the Taylor & Francis Group, an informa business

British Library Cataloguing in Publication Data
A catalogue record for this book is available from the British Library

ISBN: 978-0-367-34616-4 (Set)
ISBN: 978-0-429-34352-0 (Set) (ebk)
ISBN: 978-0-367-37002-2 (Volume 96) (hbk)
ISBN: 978-0-367-37005-3 (Volume 96) (pbk)
ISBN: 978-0-429-35232-4 (Volume 96) (ebk)

Publisher's Note
The publisher has gone to great lengths to ensure the quality of this reprint but
points out that some imperfections in the original copies may be apparent.

Disclaimer
The publisher has made every effort to trace copyright holders and would welcome
correspondence from those they have been unable to trace.

Technology Transfer: The Role of the Sci-Tech Librarian

Cynthia Steinke
Editor

The Haworth Press
New York • London

Technology Transfer: The Role of the Sci-Tech Librarian has also been published as *Science & Technology Libraries*, Volume 11, Number 2 1990.

The Haworth Press, Inc., 10 Alice Street, Binghamton, NY 13904-1580
EUROSPAN/Haworth, 3 Henrietta Street, London WC2E 8LU England

Library of Congress Cataloging-in-Publication Data

Technology transfer : the role of the sci-tech librarian / Cynthia Steinke, editor.
    p. cm.
    "Has also been published as Science & technology libraries, volume 11, number 2, 1990" — T.p. verso.
    Includes bibliographical references.
    ISBN 1-56024-116-0 (alk. paper)
    1. Technical libraries. 2. Technology transfer. 3. Scientific libraries. 4. Technology — Information services. 5. Communication of technical information. I. Steinke, Cynthia A.
Z675.T3T425 1990   90-20014
026.50285 — dc20   CIP

Technology Transfer:
The Role
of the Sci-Tech Librarian

CONTENTS

Acknowledgement

The Editor gratefully acknowledges the assistance of Ronald L. Buchan, NASA Scientific and Technical Information Facility, for his assistance in the development of this volume.

In addition to providing a contributed paper of his own, Mr. Buchan was especially helpful in identifying other contributors from the federal sector who are actively involved in technology transfer within their organizations.

Cynthia Steinke
Editor

Introduction

The term "technology transfer" became somewhat of a buzzword in the latter half of the 1980's. But as with many terms that emerge in this way, it can refer to a number of different things, rendering a precise definition especially difficult. Most people are not exactly sure what it does mean. Contributors to this volume have provided a number of definitions, explanations and illustrations of the concept. Simply put, "technology transfer" can be considered the process of getting technical knowledge, ideas, services, inventions and products from their origin to wherever they can be put to practical use.

Activities related to the transfer of technology are designed to promote the economic well-being of a nation and its citizenry. The players in the process have most typically been the federal government and industry; more recently the academic research institution has begun to play a significant role as well. Given increasing competitiveness among nations in the international marketplace, the need to quicken the pace of technology transfer has become vital.

Implicit in the transfer of technology is the transfer of knowledge. As experts in this area, it seems a particularly appropriate time to examine the role of the information specialist in the technology transfer process. This volume brings together discussions from information intermediaries associated with federal information centers, academic research institutions and in one case the large metropolitan public library.

Dr. David Woods, Director of Scientific Information for the Department of the Navy, provides a clear picture of "who's who" in the domestic technology transfer arena: agencies and organizations at the federal, state and professional levels involved in and responsible for technology transfer programs. He exhorts librarians to actively seek ways to use their considerable information retrieval prowess to serve as "links" between these agencies and the small

1

businesses, minority-run companies and non-profit organizations that aspire to develop products and services from new federal technologies.

Many people consider NASA as the birthplace of the technology transfer concept. Indeed, the programs and publications of this agency are extensive—some well-known to researchers and others less so. Buchan's article sorts out the numerous print and online services available and identifies the various regional NASA Industrial Application Centers.

In their paper, Pinelli (NASA Langley Research Center), Kennedy (Indiana University, Center for Survey Research), and Barclay (Rensselaer Polytechnic Institute) describe the conceptual framework of a NASA/DOD study underway which seeks to better understand the production, transfer and utilization of aerospace knowledge as a precursor to the rapid diffusion of that technology. The role of the aerospace librarian as information intermediary in the transfer and utilization of knowledge derived from federally funded aerospace R&D (thus completing the knowledge transfer process) will also be investigated.

As stated by Hayes, technology transfer is a "contact sport" requiring people to people contact. All of the contributors emphasize that the more active the information intermediary, the more effective the transfer process. How far they will be drawn into the transfer process depends to a large measure on their vision of the role they want to play.

Bishop (Syracuse University, School of Information Studies) and Peterson (Wear Sciences, Inc.) lead off with a paper which describes the role of information and information specialists in the promotion of technology transfer based on the findings from research conducted on the information needs and communication patterns of scientists and engineers. ACTIS, a computer-based information system to promote technology transfer in the field of tribology, is described—including the role played by the information specialist in its development.

Pensyl (MIT Libraries) examines the emerging role of academic research institutions in the technology transfer process— serving as "economic change agents" actively seeking to contribute to the well-being of the country and its citizens. Innovative user-driven services offered by the University Library's Computerized Literature Service, illustrate how the librarians as experts in the transfer of information play an active role in the technology transfer process as well.

As coordinator of the Technology Transfer Information Center at the National Agricultural Library, Hayes examines the use of technology transfer in agricultural programs to improve competitiveness of the U.S. in the global marketplace. Hayes suggests that "information specialists can assist in the technology transfer process and ultimately the Nation's economic competitiveness by understanding the subject matter and also comprehending the importance of connecting the client to the correct information in a timely manner."

Engel, Reference Librarian in the Science and Technology Department of the Carnegie Library of Pittsburgh describes how the large metropolitan public library can promote technology transfer by acting as important centers for information transfer. Her paper focuses on the types of technical materials and services most useful to the business and industrial community.

* * *

"One hundred sixty thousand years ago, a star exploded in the Large Magellanic Cloud, a galaxy of stars near our own Milky Way Galaxy. The light from that explosion, or supernova, reached Earth on February 23, 1987. Because of the size and relative nearness of the explosion, astronomers now have had an opportunity to study the brightest supernova seen from this planet in hundreds of years." So begins our Special Paper contributed by Virgil Diodato, School of Library and Information Science, University of Wisconsin, Milwaukee.

This astronomical explosion is known by various names, among them Supernova 1987A. This event was so important that it was quickly followed by an explosion of publications. Diodato's paper examines the publication patterns of the primary and secondary literature associated with this scientific happening.

Contributed sections dealing with new sci-tech reference works, developments in online searching and with recent publications relating to sci-tech libraries complete the volume.

Cynthia Steinke
Editor

Developing Information Systems for Technology Transfer: An Example from Tribology

Ann P. Bishop
Marshall B. Peterson

SUMMARY. This paper discusses the role of information in technology transfer and presents key findings from research on the information needs and communication patterns of scientists and engineers. Implications of this research for the design and management of scientific and technical information (STI) systems, including both libraries and computerized systems, are discussed. ACTIS, a computerized information system being developed to promote technology transfer in the field of tribology, is described. ACTIS is an example of a system that has been designed with the information needs and communication patterns of scientists and engineers in mind. The paper concludes with suggestions for information specialists who are trying to promote technology transfer in their organizations.

INTRODUCTION

In order to facilitate technology transfer, information specialists in R&D settings must be knowledgeable about:

- The nature of the tasks that comprise the technology transfer process
- The nature of the scientific and technical information (STI) needed by scientists, engineers, and managers to complete these tasks

---

Ann P. Bishop received an MLS from the School of Information Studies, 4-206 Center for Science and Technology, Syracuse University, Syracuse, NY 13244-4100, where she is currently a PhD candidate. Marshall B. Peterson is President of Wear Sciences, Inc., 925 Mallard Circle, Arnold, MD 21012, and served as Technical Advisor to ACTIS.

- The communication patterns that typify R&D workers' attempts to collect and use this information
- The characteristics of the information in their collections and the way that this material is organized.

Most information specialists are experts with regard to the last item in the list. They are, in other words, very knowledgeable about information "systems" that they manage and use. But they may not be as familiar with the users of these systems, with their work, their information needs, and their communication behavior. This is hardly surprising. The nature of R&D tasks and communication patterns is not usually taught in library schools. Typically, this knowledge either results from the information specialist's own background in science and technology, or is acquired on the job, as the information specialist gains experience with the work and habits of clients.

Lack of familiarity with clients' work and information seeking and use behavior can hamper the effectiveness of both information specialists and the systems they manage. It may also provoke criticism of information center operations:[1] "There are indications that information specialists do not really understand the needs of technical professionals working in the R&D setting and that solutions offered by the information sciences are inadequate, inappropriate and/or ineffectual."

To remedy this situation, information specialists can make use of existing research on technology transfer and on the information needs and communication patterns of scientists and engineers. This research provides suggestions that can help information specialists tailor systems and services to the work of their clients. The goal, of course, is to shape services to suit the needs of clients, rather than expect clients to adapt to systems unsuited to their needs.

UNDERSTANDING TECHNOLOGY TRANSFER

In order to understand the role information plays in technology transfer, it is important to understand the process of technological innovation itself. Basic task categories in technology transfer have been identified, and the range of activities that occur in each category described, by Allen et al.:[2]

- Basic Research: results in a broad range of applications or in the development of new knowledge

- Applied Research: applies basic knowledge to the solution of a particular problem and may result in the creation and evaluation of new concepts or components

- Development: combines existing concepts with new knowledge to provide a distinctly new product or process

- Technical Service: produces cost/performance improvements to, and opens new markets for, existing products or processes.

In the traditional linear model of technology transfer, basic research leads to applied research, and thence to the development, production, and marketing of commercial products. This model, however, is being replaced with nonlinear models of innovation which emphasize the constant, interactive nature of information flows and the cognitive processes that form the basis of R&D work. Ballard et al. note that:[3]

> Once the initial idea is formulated, the path to successful marketing is a long and arduous series of design, development, testing, and production phases. In effect, this is a "problem-solving R&D process," generally requiring internal generation of STI and acquisition of external STI.

A key feature of R&D is that it is generally a collaborative process, with much of the work involving team effort. The nature of collaborative work and the means of facilitating group communication and information processing is an important area of research that deserves the attention of information specialists.[4,5]

Although technology transfer is a complex process that is not yet completely understood, products and services offered by information specialists in R&D settings are more likely to match clients' needs if they are based on an understanding of basic R&D tasks and problems. One basic cause of the mismatch between information systems and R&D workers, i.e., those scientists, engineers, and others working on technological innovations, is the perception of information centers as mechanisms for the delivery of information rather than for the solution of problems. This perception, unfortunately, is frequently held by information specialists, R&D workers, and R&D management alike.

Scientists and engineers, for example, experience information needs that are not well served by current indexing practices. Scientists planning experiments may want to search the literature to find out if a particular theoretical orientation or research method has appeared in previous studies of the phenomena they intend to investigate.[6] The literature, however, is indexed primarily according to subject matter, and access to other essential aspects such as methodology or theoretical orientation is either very limited or nonexistent. The work of Liddy[7] and Trawinski[8] suggests the possibility of structuring the abstracts of scientific and technical papers that appear in online systems to reflect the problem-solving process. They suggest that online retrieval could be enhanced if users could search specific abstract components, such as "hypothesis," "method," or "solution."

The information needs of engineers are similarly specific to the nature of their work. As Breton points out, "an engineer is a problem-solver, looking for a new solution that may not have the name of a thing attached to it. He starts with the function of what he needs."[9] The need to search by device function is seldom met by current indexing practices. Breton also notes that engineers typically need information about commercial products. Such information is available in advertisements and supplier catalogs, items not typically subjected to rigorous bibliographic control in information centers. Information specialists must be both alert to the kinds of needs that stem from the nature of R&D work and adept at strategies that overcome the inherent limitations of their information systems.

Another instance of mismatch between information systems and the needs of researchers has been identified by Wilson and Farid. They assert that R&D workers are not best served by the exhaustive literature searches information specialists have been trained to provide. Of greater value would be access to tools, whether commercially- or locally-produced, that provide synthesis, analysis, and evaluation, i.e., "more reviews, more authoritative critical surveys, more compendious works of reference, more works of *haute vulgarisation* . . . ."[10] The goal should be to reduce, rather than increase, the amount of information a researcher must sift through in order to solve a particular problem or answer a particular question.

These examples are intended to illustrate the importance of understanding both the information needs of the clients and the cognitive and procedural contexts of technology transfer out of which those needs arise. Information needs cannot be optimally met unless the work which led to those needs is understood.

INFORMATION NEEDS
AND COMMUNICATION HABITS OF R&D WORKERS

The information needs and communication habits of scientists and engineers have been studied by researchers in the fields of information science, communications, and management. Garvey[11] and Allen[12] are classic texts that review the literature, discuss issues, represent major empirical work, and make recommendations related to, respectively, scientific and technical communication. These and other studies explore the impact of STI exchange on technology transfer.[2,13,14] They also investigate variations in the contribution of scientific and technical communication to different R&D tasks and differences between scientists and engineers in the selection and use of different information sources and channels.[15-18] Poole[19] compares and analyzes the results of approximately one hundred empirical studies of information use by scientists and engineers, distilling common principles from this work. Ballard et al., although they focus on Federal technology transfer, provide a good summary of general issues and current knowledge related to the role of STI in technology transfer.[3]

Key findings drawn from the literature on the role of information in technology transfer and on the information needs and communication patterns of R&D workers include:

- Frequent and diverse communication has a positive effect on the success of technological innovation.

- Both formal (i.e., reading the literature) and informal (e.g., conversations with colleagues, browsing, attending conferences) information exchanges are critical factors in technology transfer.

- Both external (i.e., with people outside the organization) and internal (i.e., among research team members or among departments within an organization) information exchanges are needed in technology transfer.

- The value of formal vs. informal and external vs. internal information varies according to the nature of the R&D task being performed.

  —Formal information is more important for scientists, while informal exchanges are more important for engineers.

  —Informal exchanges are important for keeping up with the latest scientific and technical developments and also for solving particular problems.

  —External information sources are most important for generating ideas while internal sources are most important for solving particular problems.

  —External information is more important for scientists than for engineers.

The literature makes it clear that different types of information, as well as different information channels and sources, are needed at different stages of the technology transfer process.

In addition to describing the flow of information, this literature also identifies major barriers to the successful acquisition and exchange of information:

- R&D workers do not enjoy searching for and assimilating STI, particularly through formal sources.

- Information overload and lack of information quality control inhibit the efficient and effective use of STI.

- The degree of physical and intellectual accessibility of a particular STI channel or source is the major determinant of information use.

These barriers are all associated with Zipf's "Principle of Least Effort."[19-20] This principle, when applied to information-seeking and use, asserts that people will exert the least amount of effort possible to satisfy their needs and may even go without vital information, rather than expend energy to acquire it. The outcomes, painfully obvious to many information specialists, and implications of this principle are discussed in both practitioner-oriented and research literature.[21-23]

Advances in computer and communications technologies have great potential to improve the entire technology transfer process. Computers and electronic networks can facilitate physical and intellectual access to formal STI, expand informal communication links, and encourage both internal and external information exchanges. Thus, new developments in information technology have the potential to make problem-solving more efficient and effective, and can assist in various stages of technology transfer work, such as data collection and analysis, component design, and production and marketing. Before the potential of information technology to revolutionize R&D is reached, however, serious technical, social, and political issues will need to be resolved. A number of recent studies focus on the impact of information technology on R&D in general and on the provision of STI.[24-29]

The findings from the literature presented in this section of the paper were discussed with Dr. Gerhard Baule, Director of Technology Application at the New York State Center for Advanced Technology in Computer Applications and Software Engineering.[30] Baule's views on the process of technological innovation and on the barriers confronting scientists and engineers in their attempts to access and use information were enlightening. Although recognizing the key role that information plays in all phases of technology transfer, he cautioned that categorizations such as "scientist" and "engineer" and "basic research" and "applied research" are simplistic; thus, such terms should not be used to pigeonhole the information needs of individual R&D workers. Baule confirmed the importance of informal communication, especially in establishing closer ties among people with widely divergent functions and areas of expertise, such as engineers, lawyers, and marketing staff. Information access was cited as a critical problem, particularly for entrepreneurs in small companies trying to get an innovative product into the market. Physically distant from the university, such individuals also experience social and psychological barriers in their efforts to obtain information and solve problems. Thus, they are frequently cut off from the informal contacts and broad range of expertise and resources that are critical in technology transfer.

IMPLICATIONS FOR INFORMATION SYSTEMS

The research discussed above suggests several ways in which information specialists could begin to adjust their products and services to conform to the problem-solving activities of their clients. Information systems for technology transfer should:

- Be based on an understanding of technology transfer activities and of R&D workers' information needs and communication patterns

- Provide access to the various kinds of information needed at different stages of technology transfer, e.g., facilitate access to formal STI and enhance informal communication opportunities

- Minimize physical and intellectual effort needed to locate, acquire, and use STI resources.

The next section of this paper will describe and evaluate a computerized information system that attempts to accomplish these goals. The paper will conclude with specific recommendations for information specialists.

ACTIS: A COMPUTERIZED
TRIBOLOGY INFORMATION SYSTEM

The primary goal of ACTIS (A Computerized Tribology Information System) is to facilitate technology transfer in tribology, which is the field of study devoted to lubrication and wear. The tribology R&D community is officially represented by the American Society of Mechanical Engineers' Research Committee on Tribology, whose function is to monitor and promote research, usually by identifying engineering needs and devising projects for joint industrial participation. At its regular meeting in November of 1983, a discussion was held to develop ideas for new research projects.

More cynical members suggested that since there appeared to be little use of current research results, there was little reason to undertake major efforts to produce new results which would, in all probability, not be used either. Further discussions among the members led to the conclusion that research results experienced slow diffusion since they were not in a form which could be easily used by design and material engineers. The net result of the discussion was the decision to develop a computerized tribology information system.

"Tribology" is a recently-coined word used to describe a variety of activities associated with friction, wear, lubricants, and the design and operation of a wide variety of mechanical components. Tribology is formally defined as "the science of technology of interacting surfaces in relative motion and of the practice related thereto." Important tribological components include bearings, bushings, piston rings, brakes, gears, valves, tires, and clutches. Processes associated with tribology include abrasion, erosion, friction, adhesion, wear, and surface damage. A tribologist might be an organic chemist trying to develop stable molecular compounds for high temperature oils or a mechanical engineer designing a long-life space bearing system.

In terms of the general flow of technology transfer, the tribology community can be divided into two basic groups: knowledge providers and knowledge users. The knowledge providers are the 400 to 500 scientists and engineers in the field of tribology who do R&D in government laboratories, universities, research institutions, and a few industrial research laboratories. Much of the work published in the technical literature of tribology is funded by government agencies (e.g., the Department of Defense, the Department of Energy, the Department of Commerce, and the National Science Foundation) in support of their particular missions. Much development work is carried out by industry in support of their own products, but the results of this activity are seldom reported in the technical literature.

Generally speaking, the users of tribology information are mechanical engineers, designers, and materials engineers who work in three distinct settings:

- Companies that design and build mechanical equipment or equipment components, e.g., General Electric, Caterpillar, Black & Decker

- Companies that operate mechanical equipment, e.g., US Steel, American Airlines, United Parcel Service, and the United States Navy

- Product companies that design and build trigological products such as lubricants, tribomaterials, wear resistant coatings, bearings, gears, and seals.

In the past, the information diffusion process has been from the researchers to the tribological products companies. Interesting developments in tribology were typically reported in the literature, quickly reviewed by the appropriate product companies, and then used by them to introduce cost-effective improvements into their products. These products were then sold to the manufacturers and users of mechanical equipment. For example, when researchers reported that bearing fatigue resistance improved with thinner bearing materials, bearing manufacturers quickly reduced bearing wall thickness. When researchers learned that certain additives improved the performance of carbons in vacuum and high temperature applications, carbon brush and bearing manufacturers came out with a variety of special products to exploit this development.

In recent years, however, the knowledge providers and the knowledge users have drifted apart. Companies want to make their production more cost-effective while the researchers were investigating and providing high-cost, sophisticated technological improvements. Armed with scientific instruments, analytical techniques, and high speed computers that are vastly superior to their previous resources, researchers are probing more deeply into the meaning of such tribological processes as wear, adhesion, friction, and viscosity. Although these studies provide new insights into basic phenomena, their results are difficult to apply in practice. Potential users of tribology research, on the one hand, cannot interpret or assess the significance of research results, while researchers have little knowledge of the needs of the users or of how to fulfill them.

As stated earlier, ACTIS was designed to bridge this gap: to interpret scientific results and put them in a form which could be easily understood and used by designers and material engineers who operate primarily as problem-solvers and may have little background or interest in basic tribology research. ACTIS was conceived from within the R&D community itself, and developed as a joint effort by information providers, users, and information specialists. Thus, ACTIS serves as an example of an information system based on knowledge of the information needs and communication patterns and scientists and engineers.

Description of ACTIS Components

ACTIS has been described in a number of papers.[31-35] Its designers hope that it will enhance technology transfer by providing easy, integrated access to STI needed by R&D workers and managers. Figure 1 depicts the range of prospective users of ACTIS. When completed, ACTIS will be comprised of the six databases shown in Figure 2. The components of each database, described below, facilitate access to the broad range of information needed to solve problems at various stages of R&D work. The newsletter and research-in-progress databases, for example, might spawn new research ideas, while the numeric and design databases can provide centralized access to information particularly important in the design stages of technological innovation. Finally, the product directory provides data needed by development engineers and technical service staff that, as noted earlier, are often neglected in more traditional information systems. The system facilitates access to formal information through its link to commercial bibliographic databases, while its electronic mail capabilities encourage informal communication.

The RESEARCH-IN-PROGRESS DATABASE will contain abstracts of current, unpublished tribology research being conducted by government laboratories, industry, universities, and research institutes. The initial database was developed as the result of a survey sent to 7000 individuals, identified through their membership in an appropriate technical society or their attendance at a tribology conference. The database consists of approximately 600 current projects which are updated on a yearly basis.

POTENTIAL USERS

RESEARCHERS	ENGINEERS	PURCHASING/ SUPPLY	INFORMATION SPECIALISTS
Tribologists	Component Designers	Lubricant Suppliers	Libraries
Industrial Researchers	System Designers	Product Suppliers	Information Centers
University Faculty	Lubricant Designers	Purchasing Agents	Information Vendors
Research Laboratories	Application Engineers		Information Consultants
Government Program Managers	Failure Analysts		STI System Managers
	Maintenance Engineers		

Source: Jahanmir et al. (34)

Figure 1. Potential users of computerized data and information (based on workshops and technical demonstrations)

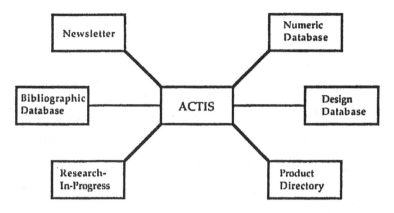

Source: Jahanmir et al. (34)

Figure 2. Schematic illustration of the six databases in ACTIS

The BIBLIOGRAPHIC DATABASE will allow tribologists, materials scientists, design engineers, information specialists, and students to search the entire range of commercial bibliographic databases (e.g., NTIS, COMPENDEX, TRIBO) covering tribology through a single point of entry or "gateway." The ACTIS gateway will help searchers find the right combination of databases, given their particular information need. Tribology researchers have noted that current indexing terms are too limited and are often incorrectly applied. Thus, an online thesaurus/glossary is being planned as part of the gateway. The thesaurus will supply links between the vocabulary of users and the indexing terms used by the various commercial databases. The ACTIS bibliographic database is also intended to serve the needs of the broad industrial community so that technology transfer can be more readily accomplished.

The NEWSLETTER DATABASE will be a communication link, consisting of a newsletter and electronic mail capabilities. It will also allow the production of a hard copy newsletter. This database will serve as an exchange mechanism for old and new technical information. The newsletter will include the latest research results in tribology, meeting notices, calls for papers, requests-for-proposals, new product announcements, book reviews, and summaries of pertinent technical topics. The reviews and summaries represent one small attempt to reduce information overload.

The NUMERIC DATABASE will consist of numeric data on the basic properties and tribological performance of materials, lubricants, components, and systems. Data in each of the areas will be critically evaluated by tribology experts who will review, distill, and compile a listing of evaluated "best-judgment" parameters and properties in a standardized format. The critical evaluation of the data eliminates, to a large degree, the need for extensive quality control on the part of information intermediaries or users themselves. (See Figure 3.)

The DESIGN DATABASE will help users design components, select materials, calculate basic parameters, develop component specifications, and diagnose failures. These data will be accessed through an expert system front-end that should facilitate its use by the non-tribologist. New developments from research can be incor-

NUMERIC DATABASE		
Materials Property Data	**Tribological Data On Material Combinations**	**Performance Data for Tribo-Components**
Metals	Lubricated Friction	Plain Bearings
Ceramics	Wear of Metal	Rolling Element Bearings
Polymers	Friction/Wear of Nonmetals	
Coatings		Gears
Composites	Abrasive Wear	Seals
Lubricants	Erosive Wear	Brakes/Clutches
Additives	Solid Lubricants & Coatings	Cutting Tools
	High Temp. Materials	

Source: Jahanmir et al. (34)

Figure 3. Three technical areas to be covered in the
numeric database, with examples

porated quickly into this database and thus put to immediate use. (See Figure 4.)

The PRODUCT AND SERVICES DIRECTORY DATABASE will identify and describe those commercially available tribology products and related services most often used by application, maintenance, design engineers and purchasing agents. The database will contain information on tribocomponents, tribosystems, materials, and lubricants, as well as available services such as consultation and maintenance.

ACTIS differs from traditional information systems in that it is intended to facilitate both formal and informal information exchanges. It brings more ephemeral material under stricter bibliographic control and offers a single point of access to this broad range of information. It also intends to offer retrieval mechanisms that are more useful and better-suited to the problem-solving needs of R&D workers.

The Development of ACTIS

The development of ACTIS began when the Tribology Program of the U.S. Department of Energy's Conservation and Utilization Technology Division decided to fund the project and assigned project responsibility to NIST (National Institute of Standards and Technology). To plan the project, a workshop was held in July 1985. The purpose of the workshop was to assess the needs for such a system, design individual databases, and plan for overall integration of the different components into one system. The workshop ran for four weeks and was attended by approximately 60 people. Equally represented were tribology specialists, information specialists, and company tribologists. The company tribologists, as the primary user group, were there to voice their needs, which they did in no uncertain terms. The tribology specialists defined the state of knowledge which could be used in such a system. The information specialists came from major international science and technology agencies, from academic and corporate science and technology libraries, and from information technology corporations and consulting firms. Chiefly information system analysts and designers, most also had science or engineering backgrounds; thus, they contributed

DESIGN DATABASE			
Design Guides	Calculations of Basic Parameters	Component Design Calculations	Failure Diagnostics
Component Selection Bearing Selection Material Selection	Contact Stress Lubricant Film Thickness Contact Temperature	Rolling Element Bearings Spur Gears Face Seals	Bearings Gears Seals

Source: Jahanmir et al. (34)

Figure 4. Four technical areas to be covered in the
design database, with examples

important knowledge about the design and use of information storage and retrieval systems. Also valuable to the project was their knowledge of existing scientific and technical information resources and their experience with a broad range of prospective users.

One recommendation resulting from the workshop was that ACTIS be developed in four phases. During the first phase, a demonstration system was developed in order to interest other possible funders. The second phase resulted in a prototype system that was developed as a means to get feedback from the broader user community before the implementation of a preliminary operational system in phase three. In the fourth phase, several of the databases will be expanded and improved, and the user interface and retrieval mechanisms will be enhanced.

Throughout the period from 1986 to 1989, the system has been developed more or less according to schedule. The preliminary operational system is currently under development. A not-for-profit corporation called ACTIS Inc., whose officers are themselves experts in the field of tribology, has been established to continue the development of the system. Still to be completed are the performance component of the numeric database and the design guides and failure diagnostics of the design database. The corporation, with funding from a variety of sponsors and from users, will continue to enlarge and enhance the system. It should be available for general use by 1991.[36]

ACTIS designers have been confronted with a number of difficulties. Although the system designers were forewarned by the information specialists, the development of a user interface has proved more complex than envisioned by the tribologists. Special care has been taken with the user interface because, as the information specialists noted, the value of the system will be limited if it is not easy to use, regardless of the quality of the data it contains. This conclusion is not unique to the ACTIS design team; the process of designing an interface based on knowledge of the information needs and information-seeking behavior of researchers in a particular field has been discussed, for example, by Borgman et al.[37]

Perhaps the most difficult problem associated with the development of the system was determining the cost effectiveness of the different databases. The tribologists, left to themselves, would have attempted to implement the most comprehensive system imaginable. But some of their ideas were impractical. For example, the tribologists wanted an online listing of all people working in the field along with their addresses, telephone numbers, and specialties. The information specialists agreed that this would be nice but questioned the practicality of such a suggestion. They asked the tribologists how much they would be willing to pay to find someone's telephone number via a central computer system? They suggested that printing and selling the directory for a small fee might be more sensible. Eventually, each database had to be reduced in scope to be cost effective. Another problem that was discussed frequently was responsibility for the quality of the data. Suppose that an engineer uses ACTIS design tools to design a bearing which subsequently fails in service. Who is responsible for the failure, and what steps need to be taken to ensure that the system represents the best current engineering judgment?

The information specialists played a vital role throughout the conceptualization and development of ACTIS. Their primary role was to keep the system within the realms of reason, in terms of both technical feasibility and practical utility. They also were of great assistance in formatting the information so it could be easily used, even by novices. They aided the tribologists in removing jargon, defining terms, explaining complex concepts, and simplifying approaches. As noted above, the information specialists also had primary responsibility for the design of the user interface. If ACTIS is successful it will be because of the close working relationship between tribologists and information specialists. The next step in the development of the system will be to collect additional feedback from actual users of the ACTIS prototype and try to incorporate their suggestions into the development of the operational system.

CONCLUSION

This paper has discussed the information needs and communication behavior of R&D workers and has highlighted some implications from current research in this area for the improvement of information systems. Because technology transfer is essentially a problem-solving activity, information systems of all kinds must help solve R&D problems rather than merely provide STI. ACTIS, a new, discipline-specific, networked information system, attempts to provide integrated access to a greater range of the STI needed to solve R&D problems than is traditionally available, and to do so in a manner that is better suited to the problem-solving needs of R&D workers. Although it is still too early to evaluate the success of ACTIS, the principles upon which it is based seem sound.

In conclusion, the authors offer a number of suggestions that may help information specialists increase their ability to facilitate technology transfer. Some specific suggestions were gleaned from the literature.[10,15,23,38] Other recommendations stem from the authors' review of ACTIS and from their own experience. Not all of the recommendations below are applicable to every situation, but they may nonetheless help information specialists concerned with technology transfer to generate new ideas about their information systems, services, and products:

- Keep abreast of the literature on scientific and technical communication in the information science and R&D management literature.

- Reevaluate information centers in terms of organization, access, range of information offered, and types of information exchanges facilitated. Are these satisfactory, given the nature of clients' problem-solving activities, information needs, and communication habits?

- Conduct such a reevaluation from the users' point of view. Instead of asking clients to evaluate the information center, ask them about their work and their attempts to solve work-related problems. Then assess the degree to which information services and resources were useful in solving these problems. Try to analyze the cause of any system failures.

- Try to attend your clients' project meetings as another means of better understanding the nature of their work and problems.

- Remember that ease of access and "user friendliness" are not just nice "extras" in the design of an information system (e.g., information center, card catalog, online database). They are critical, and will determine whether, and the degree to which, services and resources are used. Do everything in your power to make the existence of your resources known and to make them readily accessible: push for a central location for the information center; conduct open houses; use signs wherever needed; route literature, references, abstracts, and tables of contents to clients; consider an online public access catalogue so that clients can access resources from their labs and offices; and bolster bibliographic instruction. Do not assume that, just because your clients are well-educated and technically sophisticated, they will find it easy to negotiate information systems.

- Think of the information center's role as problem-solving, not simply information storage and supply. If you know more about your clients' work, you can add value to your products and services: prepare or provide critical reviews and assessments of the literature; provide in-depth bibliographic assistance; and devise means to enhance subject-only indexing and cataloging.

• Try to facilitate informal communication and information exchange among R&D workers. Informal exchange provides their chief means of getting ideas and finding out how to do things: advertise conferences; sponsor informal lectures or discussions; provide comfortable places for people to meet and talk; create internal information and referral (I&R) files that list the interests, skills, and knowledge of internal and external experts; and introduce R&D workers to electronic network services, such as bulletin boards and electronic mail, that provide access to expertise and resources well beyond the walls of the organization.

Enhancing the role of information centers and the information specialist in technology transfer is not an easy task; it involves cultural changes within the organization as a whole. It entails a revision of clients' expectations. Users must be convinced that the information specialist is not a passive provider of documents and information, but an active participant in the discovery and generation of solutions to R&D problems. With such increases in activity and understanding, benefits to the entire organization will be considerable and demonstrable. Management will be convinced that the information center is not merely an expensive luxury but is, instead, an integral and invaluable component of the organization.

REFERENCES

1. Davis, P.; Wilkof, M. Scientific and technical information transfer for high technology: Keeping the figure in its ground. *R&D Management*. 18(1): 45-58; 1988.

2. Allen, Thomas J.; Lee, Denis M.S.; Tushman, Michael L. R&D performance as a function of internal communication, project management, and the nature of work. *IEEE Transactions on Engineering Management*. EM-27(1): 2-12; 1980 Feb.

3. Ballard, Steven; James, Thomas; Adams, Timothy; Devine, Michael; Malysa, Lani; Meo, Mark. *Innovation through technical and scientific information: Government and industry cooperation*. NY: Quantum Books; 1989, 198 p.

4. Greif, I., ed. *Computer-supported cooperative work: A book of readings*. San Mateo, CA: Morgan Kaufman; 1988, 783 p.

5. Olson, Margrethe H., ed. *Technological support for work group collaboration*. Hilldale, NY: Lawrence Erlbaum Associates; 1989, 199 p.

6. Weinberg, Bella. Why indexing fails the researcher. *The Indexer*. 16 (1): 3-6; 1988 April.

7. Liddy, Elizabeth D. Discourse-level structure in abstracts. *In*: Chen, Ching-chih, ed. *Proceedings of the 50th Annual Meeting of the American Society for Information Science, Boston, Massachusetts, October 4-8, 1987 (Vol. 24)*. Medford, NJ: Learned Information; 1987, p. 138-147.

8. Trawinski, Bogdan. A methodology for writing problem structured abstracts. *Information Processing & Management*. 25 (6): 693-702; 1989.

9. Breton, Ernest. Why engineers don't use databases. *American Society for Information Science Bulletin*. p. 20-23; 1981 Aug.

10. Wilson, P.; Farid, M. On the use of the records of research. *The Library Quarterly*. 49 (2): 127-145; 1979 April.

11. Garvey, W.D. *Communication: The essence of science*. Oxford, England: Pergamon Press; 1979, 332 p.

12. Allen, Thomas J. *Managing the flow of technology: Technology transfer and the dissemination of technological information within the R&D organization*. Cambridge, MA: The MIT Press; 1984, 320 p.

13. Orpen, Christopher. The effect of managerial distribution of scientific and technical information on company performance. *R&D Management*. 15 (4): 305-308; 1985.

14. Ebadi, Yar M.; Utterback, James M. The effects of communication on technological innovation. *Management Science*. 30 (5): 572-585; 1984 May.

15. Gerstberger, Peter; Allen, Thomas J. Criteria used by research and development engineers in the selection of an information source. *Journal of Applied Psychology*. 52 (4): 272-279; 1968.

16. Gerstenfeld, Arthur; Berger, Paul. An analysis of utilization differences for scientific and technical information. *Management Science*. 26 (2): 165-179; 1980 Feb.

17. Chakrabarti, Alok; Feineman; Fuentevilla, William. Characteristics of sources, channels, and contents for scientific and technical information systems in industrial R and D. *IEEE Transactions on Engineering Management*. EM-30 (2): 83-88; 1983 May.

18. Batson, Robert. Characteristics of R&D management which influence information needs. *IEEE Transactions on Engineering Management*. EM-34 (3): 178-183; 1987 Aug.

19. Poole, Herbert L. *Theories of the middle range*. Norwood, NJ: Ablex; 1985, 159 p.

20. Zipf, George K. *Human behavior and the principle of least effort: An introduction to human ecology*. NY: Addison-Wesley; 1949.

21. Culnan, M.J. The dimensions of perceived accessibility to information: Implications for the delivery of information systems and services. *Journal of the American Society for Information Science*. 36: 302-306; 1985.

22. Bierbaum, Esther. A paradigm for the '90s. *American Libraries*. 21 (1): 18-19; 1990 Jan.

23. Cutler, W. Gale. When "Johnny" won't read. *Research Technology Management*. p. 53; 1988 September/Oct.

24. McClure, Charles R.; Bishop, Ann; Doty, Philip. *Impact of high-speed networks on scientific communication and research: Final report to the U.S. Congress, Office of Technology Assessment*. Syracuse, NY: School of Information Studies, Syracuse University; 1990 (Mimeograph).

25. Panel on Information Technology and the Conduct of Research. *Information technology and the conduct of research: The user's view*. Washington, DC: National Academy Press; 1989, 72 p.

26. U.S. Congress, Office of Technology Assessment. *Federal scientific and technical information in an electronic age: Opportunities and challenges*. OTA Staff Paper. Washington, DC: U.S. Congress, Office of Technology Assessment; 1989.

27. Lee, Soonchul; Treacy, Michael E. Information technology impacts on innovation. *R&D Management*. 18 (3): 257-271; 1988.

28. Allen, Thomas. Organizational structure, information technology, and R&D productivity. *IEEE Transactions on Engineering Management*. EM-33 (4): 212-217; 1986 Nov.

29. Case, Thomas L.; Pickett, John R. R&D information systems. *Research Technology Management*. p. 29-33; 1989 July-Aug.

30. Personal interview with Dr. Gerhard Baule, May 11, 1990.

31. Rumble, J.; Sibley, L., eds. *Towards a tribology information system*. National Bureau of Standards Special Publication 737. Washington, D.C.; U.S. Department of Commerce; 1987, 133 p.

32. Sibley, L.B.; Peterson, M.B.; and Levinson, T. An assist for tribological design. *Mechanical Engineering*. p. 68; 1986 September.

33. Danyluk, S.; Hsu, S.M. A computerized tribology information system, ACTIS. *In*: Fulton, R.E., ed. *Managing engineering data: The competitive edge: Presented at the 1987 ASME International Computers in Engineering Conference and Exhibition, August 9-13, 1987, New York, New York*. NY: American Society of Mechanical Engineers; 1987, p. 133-144.

34. Jahanmir, S.; Ruff, A.W.; Hsu, S.M. A computerized tribology information system. *In*: Blau, P.J.; Schmidt, F.A., eds. *Engineered Materials for Advanced Friction and Wear Applications*. Metals Park, Ohio: ASM International; 1988, p. 243-246.

35. Jahanmir, S.; Hsu, S.M.; Munro, R.G. ACTIS: Towards a comprehensive computerized tribology information system. *In*: Glazman, J.S.; Rumble, R.J., eds. *Computerization and Networking of Materials Data Bases, ASTM STP 1017*. Philadelphia, PA: American Society for Testing and Materials; 1989; p. 340-348.

36. Personal interview with Allan Hughes, Executive Director of ACTIS. For further information about the availability of ACTIS, contact Hughes at: (302) 998-8240.

37. Borgman, Christine L; Case, Donald O.; Meadow, Charles T. The design and evaluation of a front—end user interface for energy researchers. *Journal of the American Society for Information Science*. 40(2): 99-107; 1989 March.

38. Walton, Kenneth; Dismukes, John; Browning, Jon E. An information specialist joins the R&D team. *Research Technology Management*. p. 32-37; 1989 September/Oct.

Emerging Roles for Academic Librarians in the Technology Transfer Process

Mary Pensyl

SUMMARY. Within the past decade the university has taken on a new role in technology transfer and economic development. Implicit in the transfer of technology is the transfer of information, which affords new roles and opportunities for the information specialist. This paper describes innovative and user-driven uses of commercial databases for technology transfer at the Computerized Literature Search Service, a unit of the Massachusetts Institute of Technology (MIT) Libraries.

Universities — particularly research institutions — have long been involved in the transfer of academic research results to the public sector. Until the last decade, however, this transfer has been largely accomplished by traditional and passive methods, such as the publication of books and articles; the presentation of scholarly papers at scientific conferences; faculty consulting; and formal and informal contact with colleagues.

Within the past ten years a new academic culture has emerged with regard to technology transfer. Changes in federal policies, as well as new government programs designed to increase American productivity, have spurred universities to initiate many types of formal programs to promote the commercialization of their research results. These programs range from university joint ventures and

Mary Pensyl is Head, Computerized Literature Search Service, MIT Libraries, 14S-M48, Massachusetts Institute of Technology, 77 Massachusetts Avenue, Cambridge, MA 02139. She received a BA from Chatham College, Pittsburgh, and an MA and MLS from Simmons College, Boston.

The author would like to thank Susan N. Bjørner and Debra Silverman for their help in the preparation of this paper.

research consortia to industrial liaison programs to in-house patent and technology licensing offices.[1] Donald R. Baldwin, the director of the Technology Transfer Office at the University of Washington has written:

> The evolution of this new role for universities in economic development is one of the most interesting to occur in the academic community in many years and may be one of the most important, too, given its potential contribution to the wellbeing of the country and its citizens.[2]

In addition to formal programs, academic support for technology transfer has traditionally included resources such as laboratory facilities, computer centers, interdisciplinary programs and centers, and research consortia. Other important but frequently overlooked resources in this endeavor are the library and the academic librarian/information specialist.

Since implicit in the process of technology transfer is the transfer of information, academia's expanding role in this process affords new challenges and opportunities for information professionals. As experts in the transfer of information, librarians can assist universities in their new role as economic change agents by taking the initiative in promoting information awareness, assessing information needs, and implementing appropriate and customized value-added services to meet them:

> If the United States is to become more competitive and devise innovative ways to improve the dissemination of information and to develop policies that assist U.S. firms, scientists, and others in tapping foreign markets, we must better understand information gathering behavior and the values attached to different information resources. Information systems must be molded to fit the expectation of users, not vice versa.[3]

When information is perceived as a resource, it follows that those whose expertise is locating, filtering, interpreting, and delivering it in a timely manner are central to the process. To be most successful, however, the information professional must be perceived as an integral part of the technology transfer mission:

The improved information tools — computer, telecommunication, and new optical disk technologies — now permit information managers to consider the entire system and define how information can best be transmitted . . . . How fast this involvement will come is uncertain. It took practically a generation after the introduction of computers before senior management of the most sophisticated companies began to view information as a resource. Managers . . . still do not realize the breadth of information needed to transplant technology, the expense of gathering information, or the cost of not having sufficient information.[4]

Although many in academe still regard librarians in traditional ways, do not understand what information professionals can do for them, and are not attuned to the idea of information as a key component in technology transfer, there are signs that this is changing. At the Massachusetts Institute of Technology (MIT) faculty and researchers involved in information-intensive activities are increasingly recognizing the need for information support and are seeking guidance from professionals.

User-initiated requests have resulted in several unique and innovative uses of the Computerized Literature Search Service (CLSS), a fee-based unit of the MIT Libraries. Foremost among these are the gathering of information relevant to the issuance and safeguarding of patents, and the employment of bibliometric techniques to study emerging areas of technology.

PATENT ISSUANCE AND INFRINGEMENT

Patents have long been recognized as a major vehicle for the transfer of technology. Critical to the new role of academia in fostering economic development have been a number of changes in U.S. patent law. With the passage of PL96-517 in 1980, and subsequent amendments, Congress gave universities the right to ownership of patents developed by them under federal funding. Deliberately aimed at stimulating technological development and quickening the flow of research results into the marketplace, the act catalyzed universities to identify and license innovations developed in their research facilities.

The new profit incentives, as well as clarification of title rights and renewal of licensing restrictions, galvanized patent activity in public and private institutions. While a total of 619 patents were issued to universities in 1986, the number grew to 1,145 in 1989. That year MIT led all universities, receiving 102 patents.[5]

While many universities use outside patent agencies to facilitate the transfer and licensing of inventions, others with a long tradition of entrepreneurial activity, such as MIT and Stanford, maintain internal patent and technology licensing offices for that purpose. For several years CLSS has worked closely with the Institute's Technology Licensing Office.

For each patent application filed at MIT, an online search is required. Originally, such literature scans were conducted by legal firms; however, after a comparison was made of the results of searches performed by CLSS and by the outside firms, it was determined that the "in-house" searches were comparable to or better than those done off-campus and were generally less expensive.

Furthermore, the CLSS searches were found to offer the additional advantage that the inventors could be present during the search process—a mode of operation that exploits the advantages of the interactive capabilities of online searching. The librarian's ability to modify and refine the search as it progresses, based on first-hand input from the user, is invaluable. Clients provide essential guidance, and are available to validate results on cutting-edge research topics. An added benefit is the extended personal contact between user and searcher, which develops professional rapport and collegial dialog.

Clients of CLSS are requested either to prepare a user problem statement or provide a copy of their disclosure at the time of their search appointment, which includes both a literature search and a patent review. If a previous patent of interest is known, a cited patent search is also performed. The Technology Licensing Office recognizes that these searches cannot be exhaustive, but it nevertheless finds them valuable in deciding whether to pursue or abandon cases.

The infringement of patents is a growing concern for universities as well as industry. Today, huge sums of money ride on the outcome of cases pertaining to the violation of patents.[6] CLSS has investigated several cases involving the possible infringement of MIT patents. Ordinarily, the first technique employed is to check whether any recent patents have directly cited the specific known MIT patent.

Another method, for testing less obvious but possible violations, is to search highly significant subject terms occurring in journal literature and limit them to publications from companies. The patent holder then reviews the retrieved papers to evaluate whether infringement could be argued.

The use of commercial science, technology, and patent databases to obtain up-to-date information is clearly valuable to the MIT community and supports the goals of technology transfer. But the use of these databases for information gathering and answering specific questions is only one way that online services have assisted this process. Other, less traditional uses have evolved as a result of user needs and the increasing level of information awareness percolating through the user community.

BIBLIOMETRICS

Another frequently requested and sophisticated use of online databases has been for bibliometric analysis of patent and literature citations, particularly as a means for determining long-term trends in technology. Bibliometrics was an important research tool for the analysis of publication trends even before the advent of the computer. Significant work in forecasting emerging technologies and assessing their competitive positions has been done by the Battelle Pacific Northwest Laboratories, which developed more than 60 indicators that could be applied to a group of patents to assess the prospects of a technology.[7] Further refinements of the technique have led to its use in strategic planning and new venture evaluation.[8]

It has been noted that patent and licensing systems are also information systems:

The patent systems of the world contain a vast, long-running and detailed record of inventive activity which was extremely inaccessible prior to the advent of computers. Over the last decade, the application of new methods of information storage and retrieval to patent systems has begun to open up this storehouse of information to researchers in various areas. . . . [9]

With the advent of commercial online systems, this vast storehouse of information has come to be within the reach of anyone who has a modem and a password—becoming, in essence, "a research tool for everyman."[10] Online bibliometrics can be applied to virtually any database and thus constitutes a research technique of great significance to those aware of its potential. Distributions by various subsets of fields of information, such as countries, authors, and journal titles, make it possible to track trends, identify experts and highly published authors, and map R&D activity and technological developments.

Researchers from the Management of Technology Group at MIT's Sloan School of Management have worked with the CLSS staff on several large-scale bibliometric projects. Assuming that commercial online databases could be used for analytic purposes, researchers sought out the service and worked closely with the intermediaries in defining the parameters of a series of studies on various technologies.[11,12]

In several cases, the researchers came prepared with previously identified keywords and names of specific inventors and companies to be investigated. Usually searches were requested in tagged record format so that the information could be downloaded into a local database for analysis and the eventual generation of a model of a specific technology.

Frequently the searches were iterative, and took a number of weeks to complete. For example, a search of the patent literature to analyze several generations of integrated circuit technologies required: (a) the scanning of abbreviated titles to ascertain relevance, followed by the printing out of the full abstracts of selected items; (b) refining the listing of relevant patents yet again and then searching on the patents cited by the winnowed list; (c) printing the title of the cited patents for selection and duplicate detection; and (d) printing full abstracts of the selected set.

For one client, extensive searches were conducted on the IN-SPEC database. Emerging technologies such as neural networks and high temperature superconducting materials were examined to determine major players and how the technologies had developed over time. After the number of citations was determined (usually two or three thousand), the searchers downloaded them as tagged full records. The researchers then loaded the records into a temporary local ProCite database and manipulated and analyzed them by numerous criteria, such as author affiliation, and date and source of publication.

The extensive time, labor, and computer costs involved in this procedure led to exploration of ways to make the process more efficient. The GET command, available on the ORBIT system and originally developed for patent applications, was investigated for several of these searches. This powerful command ranks and sorts information by various criteria for quick statistical analyses of selected record fields.[13]

In another case, CLSS saved retrieval time through the researcher's purchase of a vendor password and communications software package. This option enabled the researcher to download directly records sent to him by the searcher via Dialmail, an overnight document delivery capability.

Should the researcher desire to take over the searching as well as the downloading process, he could purchase his own account on Dialog's Knowledge Index. Then either he or a graduate student could enter search strategy, and download directly into a local database, thereby reducing direct costs and removing the necessity of reserving time on CLSS computers for the large-scale computer sessions. It is likely, however, that librarian assistance would continue to be sought in developing and confirming search strategy and output techniques.

RESEARCH PARTNERSHIPS

These collaborative efforts also led to an application for a Council on Library Resources Cooperative Research Grant, which was awarded jointly to one of the search intermediaries and two researchers. The grant will provide the opportunity to further test computer literature searching as a technique for gathering and analyzing information about the development of a particular technology and the constituency of its research community. The search intermediary will provide general information support, search strategy development, and analysis of search results.

Throughout these searches, clients and intermediaries worked as a team. The researchers evinced no desire to learn the arcane mysteries of online retrieval themselves, preferring instead to consult the searchers for advice on the best way to go about locating and analyzing the information needed for their projects. Through involvement with the researchers' work, the searchers advanced their own skills and knowledge, experimenting out of necessity with often esoteric methods of retrieving and "outputting" the desired information in the most cost-effective way.

SKILL SETS INVOLVED
IN THE EFFECTIVE TRANSFER OF INFORMATION

Clients' needs in this case were met by the arsenal of "specialized knowledge" which most contemporary science and technology research librarians take for granted, but which is nonetheless unique. This repertoire includes: (a) training in the analysis of the information problem; (b) intellectual search formulation and design; (c) knowledge of patents and their organization; (d) knowledge of the literature of science and technology in printed and online form; (e) extensive online experience with multiple vendors; (f) general experience with databases and their arrangement; (g) facility with specialized search software; (h) awareness of where to go for help; (i) ability to validate both the search process and results; and (j) professional interest and understanding.

It seems clear that researchers who have complex information needs are increasingly aware of the potential of the new and emerging information tools and are desirous of utilizing them. The information specialist, who possesses the know-how and training to exploit these tools, is a natural—though not always obvious—choice as research partner. In the information age, customized research is at the heart of the "new" librarian's role. As Miriam Drake has observed:

Service in the process or management mode is similar to the work of an attorney or physician and relies on the use of specialized knowledge, education, experience, interpersonal communication, and data to help a client solve a problem.[14]

Collaborative and closer working relationships with faculty and researchers is also in keeping with the mission of major research libraries. The MIT Libraries' Strategic Plan delineates an evolving staff role for librarians as "information guides":

By the beginning of the 21st Century, the librarian will have become a more essential guide through the increasingly complex maze of information. Librarians will combine their subject knowledge with their skills in developing databases, designing retrieval systems, and organizing service to find the particular, book, data, or image that meets the MIT user's need. Librarians will have strengthened their working relationships with members of the MIT community and, through assistance in the identification and evaluation of information sources, contributed to the productivity of scholars and researchers . . . . [15]

As universities become more cognizant of the importance of information in the technology transfer mission, they will come to more fully value and utilize the skills of one of their most important allies in that process—the information professional.

REFERENCES

1. Trends in technology transfer at Universities. *Report of the Clearinghouse on University-Industry Relations*. Washington, D.C.: Association of American Colleges; 1986 Jul.; 61 p. Available from: ERIC, Washington, D.C.; ED 281398.

2. Baldwin, Donald R. Academia's New Role in Technology Transfer and Economic Development. *Research Management Review*. 2(2):15; 1988 Fall.

3. Hernon, Peter. The role of U.S. libraries and information centers in fostering competitiveness. *Government Information Quarterly*, 6(1): 52; 1989.

4. Farkas-Conn, Irene S. Human aspects of information management for technology transfer. *Information Management Review*, 4(2): 54; 1988 Fall.

5. Patent productivity picks up. *The MIT Report*. 18(3): 2; 1990 Apr.

6. Alster, Norman. New profits from patents. *Fortune*, 117(9): 185-190; 1988 Apr.

7. Campbell, Richard S. Patenting the future: a new way to forecast changing technology. *The Futurist*. 17(2): 62-67; 1983 Dec.

8. Ashton, W. Bradford; Sen, Rajat K. Using patent information in technology business planning - 1. *Research-Technology Management*. 31(6): 42-46; 1988 Nov.-Dec.

9. Kingston, Diana. Patents, licenses, and technology transfer. *Lasie*. 17(6): 142; 1987 May-Jun.

10. Persson, O. Online bibliometrics, a tool for every man. *Scientometrics*. 10(1-2): 69-75; 1986.

11. Rappa, Michael A. Bibliometric methods for monitoring the emergence of new technologies. *MIT Sloan School of Management Working Paper #3049-89-BPS*; 1989 Jul.

12. Rappa, Michael A. The dynamics of R & D communities: implications for technology strategy. *MIT Sloan School of Management Working Paper #3023-89-BPS*; 1989 Jun.

13. Bjørner, Susan N. Overcoming the fear of getting: Orbit's Get command for first-time users. *Online*. 14(4): 90-93; 1990 Jul.

14. Drake, Miriam A. Management of information. *College and Research Libraries*. 50(5): 529; 1989 Sep.

15. *The MIT Libraries at the beginning of the 21st century—a strategic plan*. Cambridge, MA: The Libraries, Massachusetts Institute of Technology; 1988 Dec.

American Libraries
and Domestic Technology Transfer

David L. Woods

SUMMARY. A lot of useful technology is being developed within the nearly 400 Federal research and development laboratories. Many Federal, state, regional, and local arms of government along with various activities within the private section are trying to help private sector organizations gain access to this Federal technology by means of licenses or other appropriate use of Federal R&D resources. This task is complicated by the facts that government labs are not used to "selling" developments and the spectrum is too large for "one-stop shopping" by most private organizations. U.S. libraries can assist in providing access to this technological data, particularly for small business ventures, via electronic data bases or other innovative techniques.

One of the more popular topics in certain governmental, industrial, and economic circles today is technology transfer. At the beginning, however, it is necessary to eliminate one common misconception. Most knowlegeable individuals assume "technology transfer" is what takes place when one nation copies without permission a vehicle or system (such as an airplane) of another nation.

David L. Woods is Director of Scientific Information for the Department of the Navy based at the Office of Naval Technology. He holds an AB in Speech from San Jose State College, an MA in Mass Media from Stanford University, an MBA in Management from Rollins College, and a PhD in Communication from The Ohio State University. In early 1987, he founded DaleWood Enterprises, Inc. and serves as CEO and President of this magazine/newsletter publishing and advertising firm.

This article expresses personal opinion. It does not represent any official policies of the Department of the Navy, the Department of Defense, nor the Administrative Branch of the Federal Government.

This is correct as far as it goes. And even in these days of a warming cold war, examples of such activity abound—particularly in military technology. But while this situation does represent technology transfer, it is NOT "domestic" technology transfer. Such unauthorized use is more accurately illegal international technology transfer.

Domestic technology transfer, in contrast, refers to legal use by some private sector organization of unclassified technology developed within a Federal research and development laboratory. Thanks to the Congress of the United States, public technology is now available (via license) for use by all manner of private sector organizations.

Authority for such actions derives from Public Law 96-480 (The Stevenson-Wydler Technology Innovation Act of 1989) as amended by Public Law 99-502 (The Federal Technology Transfer Act of 1986) and the technology competitiveness section of Public Law 100-418 (The Omnibus Trade and Competitiveness Act). Executive Order 12591 of 10 April 1987 (Facilitating Access to Science and Technology) provides additional guidance on this general topic and relates technology transfer to Public Law 98-620 (The Trademark Clarification Act of 1984) and Public Law 96-517 (The Small Business Patent Procedure Act of 1980).

Reduced to the minimum, all these acts and orders praise both Federal technology along with American science and invention, and urge combining these two forces by means of domestic technology transfer. For at least several decades, some observers have predicted lofty goals for domestic technology transfer, such as reducing the Federal budget, providing more jobs for American citizens, helping rejuvenate depressed areas, improving our balance of trade, rewarding intellectual talents, renewing the Americal Industrial base—indeed, ultimately strengthening the entire nation both economically and technologically.

At the same time, more critical observers have compared domestic technology transfer to a massive "singles" dating bureau. A long line of industrial, academic, non-profit, small business, and local, regional, and state organizations with growing technological needs stand along one side of this make-believe ballroom, while the other side reveals a gaggle of talented Federal laboratory inventors with useful, innovative, and available Federal technology.

PLAYERS IN FEDERAL DOMESTIC TECHNOLOGY TRANSFER

The core of all Federal domestic technology transfer is formed by nearly 400 Federal laboratories. Fourteen Federal agencies have one or more activities with a mission of research and development. The Departments of Defense and Energy as well as the National Aeronautics and Space Administration operate many well-known laboratories, however other departments, such as Agriculture, Health and Welfare, and Interior also include laboratories producing myriad technology potentially useful for private tasks — as well as for the public tasks for which it evolved in the first place.

Key provisions in enabling Federal technology transfer legislation permit a government laboratory to receive and retain the funds received from commercial licenses for use of technology invented by the laboratory. The actual inventor (or inventors) is also granted at least 15% of this income. Each agency may increase the share given that agency's inventors. This is 20% within the Department of the Navy, although some Federal agencies permit up to 50% of the income received from commercial licenses to be passed back to the inventor(s). Those who invented the AIDS vaccine have reportedly received the maximum amount permitted, $100,000 per year.

The package of legislation cited earlier also provided official recognition to a Federal Laboratory Consortium for Technology Transfer (FLC) composed of members of the Congressionally-mandated Office of Research and Technology Applications (ORTA) and other Federal employees at each such laboratory with interest in, or responsibility for, domestic technology transfer.

The FLC was organized in 1974 and formally chartered by the Federal Technology Act of 1986. In essence, the FLC is a service organization linking individual laboratory members with potential users of government-developed technology. The FLC holds two annual meetings, sponsors or co-sponsors various other meetings, has a network of six regional coordinators, operates an informational clearinghouse, gives awards to individuals for technology transfer excellence, operates committees that try to improve the technology transfer process, and generally assists technology transfer efforts wherever possible. For the past several years, the FLC has been funded directly by the 14 Federal agencies. Each contributes a share of its R&D budget now adding up to about $1M annually.

The Department of Commerce is the lead Federal agency for technology transfer. Its National Institute of Standards and Technology (NIST), formerly the National Bureau of Standards, located in Gaithersburg, MD, has significant new responsibilities provided by recent legislation. The primary new NIST task is setting-up an effective national program, coordinated through state and local technology outreach organizations, to place Federal technology in the private sector, particularly small business enterprises. Another portion of Commerce, the National Technical Information Service (NTIS), based in Springfield, VA provides a range of information service from on-line data bases to hard copy documents and directories.

Among other Federal agencies, a special Technology Utilization program is run by the National Aeronautics and Space Administration (NASA) from its Washington, DC headquarters. The Department of Energy maintains an information center for technical transfer information at P.O. Box 62, Oak Ridge, TN 37831. It also may be of interest that the initial technology transfer act separated the Departments of the Army, Navy, and Air Force from their parent Department of Defense for purposes of domestic technology transfer. Thus, four of the 14 Federal agencies in this program are military.

Many states, regions, and even some cities or counties also have established organizations that are very supportive of technology transfer, even if not totally devoted to that end. Most of these groups try to attract, or expand, new small business and industry in their area by helping them harness high technology. The Mississippi Technology Transfer Office located at the state-funded Mississippi Technology Transfer Center (Stennis Space Center, MS), Oklahoma Vocational Technical Schools (Stillwater, OK), and the New Mexico Research and Development Institute (Albuquerque, NM) are three active examples of different approaches to this common challenge.

Neither American industry nor small business has yet grouped nor structured itself to benefit from Federal technology transfer with ease. There are, however, a growing number of private, academic, and non-profit organizations willing to serve as "brokers" for technology. Most will either seek specific Federal technology to meet a sponsor need, or will assist a given Federal laboratory or laboratories in expanding its own marketing efforts. Some of these groups publish newletters, maintain data bases, sponsor meetings, or perform several of these functions. Either individual entrepreneurs or a cadre of venture capitalists may seek to buy or invest in small firms that have already obtained or invented new technology, rather than dealing with the government inventor or laboratory directly. Usually a "broker" is employed by such individuals or groups, although this is a monetary broker—not the technology broker noted previously.

PROFESSIONAL ASSOCIATIONS
IN TECH TRANSFER

There are two large organizations in this field, aside from the FLC. The Technology Transfer Society includes both corporate and individual members. A headquarters is maintained in Indianapolis, and the group publishes *T'Squared* a monthly newsletter and a periodic *Journal of Technology Transfer*. T² also sponsors meetings — including an annual conference. This international organization has considerable interest in overseas activity. (This is in contrast to the FLC, which is directed by Congressional legislation to give preference to American firms located in the United States.)

Another international organization is the Licensing Executives Society. This group began in 1973, and has at least 25 nations represented in LES membership. Many members are attorneys, and the various meetings sponsored by this society (including the three-day annual meeting) normally are held in international resort locations with accompanying higher costs. A quarterly journal called *Les Nouvelles* is published in English along with a newsletter titled *Les News*. LES is a worldwide federation of business-oriented, professional societies of individuals involved in the transfer of technology and industrial or intellectual property rights, and maintains its US/ Canadian headquarters in Cleveland, OH.

METHODS FOR TRANSFERRING TECHNOLOGY

Most technology transfer activity falls into four areas: (1) personal networking, (2) searching data bases, (3) group meetings, and (4) publications. Occasional gatherings may permit some one-on-one discussions between inventors and those seeking technology, but this remains fairly rare. The FLC sponsors some smaller meetings that attempt to attract both lab reps and industry technology seekers. The Department of the Navy held a Technology TransFair in Kansas City last August in which some 40 Navy inventors exchanged concepts with 100 private sector representatives. The Navy, NASA/Lewis (in Cleveland), and the Bureau of Mines plan a Great Lakes Technological Conference in Cleveland, OH on 16-17 October 1990. Such two-way events remain somewhat unusual, however.

Clearly searching data bases and using publications are activities that are far from unfamiliar to librarians. In addition, networking among data bases (in contrast to networking among individuals) also would seem to be an appropriate endeavor for a library to undertake.

Indeed, it is this black hole of technology transfer information, that so hurts progress in this field. Those seeking Federal technology need to obtain correct information, and they need it rapidly. Such information must be readily accessible in order for potential users to analyze it in advance for suitability. Yet, there is no substitute for getting a user and an inventor together. The record indicates it is unlikely much Federal technology will be transferred unless that all-essential step takes place.

Federal Technology Transfer Success

Opinions vary widely on the success of transferring Federal technology into the private sector thus far. A House of Representatives study, "Obstacles to Technology Transfer and Commercialization at Federal Laboratories" (101-31), released in October 1989, was summarized in the *Wall Street Journal* as concluding: "Technology transfer between federal labs and business is a flop so far. That's the conclusion of a report on the government's three-year-old program to help businesses commercialize federal technology. The effort has resulted in 'frustrated scientists who can't commercialize on their inventions and discouraged businessmen who can't get at valuable technologies' says a staff report prepared for Representative Ron Wyden, chairman of a House Small Business Committee." Wyden, a 5th-term Democrat, represents Oregon's 3rd District, which includes much of Portland. His small business subcommittee is the Regulation, Business Opportunities, and Energy subcommittee. The opening witness Robert Brumley III, a former government official, added: "The rub is scientists and researchers aren't businessmen and don't see the commercial value of their inventions."

A more positive view was provided by Dr. D. A. Bromley, Director of the White House Office of Science and Technology Policy, who testified 5 October 1989 at this same hearing before the Regulation, Business Opportunities, and Energy subcommittee of the House Small Business Committee. Bromley stated: "The first, and most critical step, in technology transfer is that the potential providers and potential users of technology must be brought together . . . bringing people and organizations together so that they can discover each other, remains the foremost challenge and one that we must continue to stimulate. If we're successful in linking innovators in our federal laboratories to entrepreneurs in business, they will make the technology transfer process work."

CAN LIBRARIES HELP TECHNOLOGY TRANSFER WORK?

While libraries can hardly be expected to bring inventors and business people together face-to-face, libraries offer great potential in helping fill this technology transfer information void. Both information brokers and specialized newsletters are expensive, and unlikely to be used by many small businesses—who are generally assumed to be the most likely initial users of government technology. Yet U.S. libraries, particularly those with some technical orientation, appear to provide a very helpful alternative.

If there is a sure-fire, universal data base for technology transfer, no one has yet heard of it. But there is a plethora of data bases. At a recent FLC meeting, one speaker reported a project to prepare a data base of technology transfer data bases.

These vast amounts of information exist, but only a small portion of it is useable. Who better than a librarian could help? Who else has made a successful practice of finding needles in haystacks for many years? Also, technological growth has brought us to new levels of efficiency in processing masses of data and information.

Bear in mind I am no librarian, but I have been a user. In the 1950's and early 1960's I used library card catalogs, stacks, and carrels for several years graduate work including two master's theses. A decade later, while completing an extensive dissertation involving technical history, new technology permitted me to use libraries only for initial research, to find books and documents, and for inter-library loan. I then obtained copies of virtually all required articles and sections of key books, which I was able to bring home for use at leisure. I followed a similar strategy subsequently in conducting research and publishing several books.

Since the late 1980's, I have found myself able to enter small bits of information into my Mac II or Mac Plus, print it all out, review and revise, and then quickly re-arrange this material via computer "cut and paste." Today I am able to cover more material and prepare higher quality copy with far greater speed than ever before. If an untrained hacker like myself can do this well, what of a skilled, trained librarian with the proper information and equipment?

With the right electronic or computer-based assistance, informational tasks that formerly were nearly impossible can be carried out with comparative ease. I have no doubt but that today's librarian can locate, manipulate, and distribute today's data at far less cost and with much greater speed than previously.

Thus, I believe U.S. libraries could, and should, help domestic technology transfer. Such involvement should be real-world, and should assist in particular small businesses, minority-run companies, and non-profit organizations—all of whom seem more willing to do the spadework and take the risks that developing products and services from new Federal technologies require. There is no way to tell whether or not the world will beat a path to your library, but I will bet at least one or two family jewels that any library able to develop a user-friendly method of providing useful information on domestic Federal technology transfer will gain considerable usage and the undying gratitude of many — to say nothing of helping make some of those long-predicted national dreams turn into reality. And isn't helping to "make things happen" what libraries are all about anyway? At least, I've always thought so, and hope there are a few among you who agree.

Technology Transfer at NASA —
A Librarian's View

Ronald L. Buchan

SUMMARY. There are many roles and persons responsible for effective technology transfer at NASA. The NASA Technology Utilization Division is primarily responsible for technology transfer and it's role is described. The role of "Spinoff" and "NASA Tech Briefs" are cornerstones in a program to make NASA's technology available. The librarian's role is to bring together all of the information resources that come to bear on a topic, including NASA/RECON and ARIN. The added ingredient of a librarian in the technology transfer picture expands the horizon of inquiry beyond traditional technology transfer. At the same time, when a librarian is exposed to technology transfer programs, it enhances his/her usefulness to patrons beyond traditional library science limits.

For more than twenty-five years the NASA Scientific and Technical Information Facility has been providing information to users around the globe. It is currently under the direction of the NASA Office of Management, NASA Scientific and Technical Information Division. Other NASA offices specifically interested in applying NASA's technology to both the private and government sectors are the Technology Utilization Division, the Office of Commercial Programs and the Office of Small Business and Disadvantaged Business Utilization. In addition, most NASA and contractor publications are available from the National Technical Information Service (NTIS). Information dissemination takes place in many ways

Ronald L. Buchan has a BA from Concordia College, Fort Wayne, IN, and an MLS from Pratt Institute, Brooklyn, NY. He is Lexicographer in charge of the NASA Thesaurus at the NASA Scientific and Technical Information Facility operated by RMS Associates, P.O. Box 8757, BWI Airport, MD 21240. (No copyright protection is asserted for this article.)

49

at NASA. Librarians who better understand aerospace technology transfer can improve their service to patrons.

TECHNOLOGY TRANSFER AND TECHNOLOGY UTILIZATION – DEFINITIONS

The term 'Technology Transfer' has a variety of meanings and usages. In its broadest sense 'Technology Transfer' is the identification and use of scientifically and technologically useful information. In this broad view, scientific and technical libraries are engaged in 'Technology Transfer.' The "identification" of information in this sense is equivalent to searching and the "use" or potential use can be equated with selective dissemination of information (SDI). Often the term 'Technology Transfer' is used in a more narrow sense, such as the transfer of an agency's scientific and technical information or in a still more narrow sense of specific technological developments that have business potential. Often the business of 'Technology Transfer,' in a narrow sense, is carried out by specialists who are nonlibrarians. The librarian, however, performs valuable 'Technology Transfer' functions without calling them by that name. There are other distinct meanings of 'Technology Transfer' other than the basic meanings already described. The transfer of technology to developing nations is often treated in a separate category. Many use the term to describe the utilization of foreign technology, notably European and Japanese by their own country. A lesser used sense of 'Technology Transfer' is when technology is illegally transferred to another foreign country.

The proven potential of the transfer of technology is known as 'Technology Utilization.' Many times the focus of 'Technology Transfer' is considered to be solely 'Technology Utilization.' By 1985 more than 30,000 known secondary applications of NASA Technology had been identified. These applications are real examples of 'Technology Utilization' that show the spinoffs of NASA technology. NASA's *Spinoff* publication, treated later, focuses on 'Technology Utilization.'

CORPORATE SOURCES

Not only does NASA provide information, it gives the aerospace community the chance to have pertinent information included in NASA/RECON, NASA's online information system. Over 75% of the corporate source entries for 1989 were businesses, nearly 25% of which were foreign. About 20,000 of the over 30,000 corporate sources are businesses. Although all of these companies produce literature of aerospace interest, they may also be engaged in other economic pursuits. Just as companies that input into the system have varied interests, companies with no aerospace interest may find valuable information in NASA's information products.

NASA/RECON, NTIS
AND THE AEROSPACE DATABASE

NASA/RECON, the government's first large online retrieval system, consists of 29 files organized into 17 file collections that are of aerospace interest. The two main files of NASA/RECON are online versions of two pivotal aerospace abstract journals. *Scientific and Technical Aerospace Reports* (STAR) is published by NASA for report literature. *International Aerospace Abstracts* (IAA) is published by the American Institute of Aeronautics and Astronautics as a companion to STAR. It covers journal, book, and commercial conference literature. The National Technical Information Service (NTIS) Bibliographical Database includes the STAR citations in both the online and CD-ROM versions (current only). NTIS products only list NASA items that are available from NTIS. Such items as University Microfilms dissertations of aerospace interest found in STAR are not listed in NTIS.

The online version of STAR and IAA is also publicly accessible in one continuous file since 1962 as the Aerospace Database. Both the STAR file and the IAA file are made available through AIAA on Dialog. The Aerospace Database offers Dialog features such as a small stopword list and foreign language manipulation capability. The European Space Agency/Information Retrieval Service (ESA/IRS) also has a file which is equivalent to the Aerospace Database.

Space Commercialization and File

'Space Commercialization' like 'Technology Transfer' has many meanings. The thrust of 'Space Commercialization' is 'for profit' activity in the space sector beyond contracts and grants. Thus, business activity in the space arena is seen as commercially viable. Such activity is often aided by 'Technology Transfer' and has participated in 'Technology Utilization.' The incentive for development rests with a single company or group of companies.

You can search the term 'Space Commercialization' on NASA/RECON and get over 23,000 hits, including 9,000 hits that can be retrieved from the NASA/RECON Space Commercialization file which supplements the STAR and IAA files. The Space Commercialization file is sponsored by NASA's Technology Utilization Division. Space Commercialization references are most valuable to businesses that wish to avail themselves of the opportunity to participate in space ventures.

COSMIC and Other Files

NASA has also developed many computer programs that are available publicly at prices lower than developement costs. An annual catalog of these programs is available from the Computer Software Management and Information Center (COSMIC) at the University of Georgia. The COSMIC file may also be searched online on NASA/RECON. NASTRAN is probably the most widely known and used NASA computer program and is available in many different versions. More than 1,000 articles, books and reports have been written about the NASA-developed structural engineering program and its many applications. NASTRAN stands for NAsa STRuctural ANalysis.

NASA/RECON includes other files: work in progress files, ASRDI safety files, Historical file of the National Advisory Committee for nautics (NASA's chief forerunner), limited files, older material files, and the book and periodical files of the NASA Library Network. NASA/RECON offers over 3 million records, a million more than are found on the Aerospace Database. Details of such files are often known only to librarians who regularly use NASA/RECON.

Company Information and Technology Transfer

Nearly 17,000 journal articles, reports, and books can be found in NASA/RECON under the NASA Thesaurus terms 'Technology Utilization' and 'Technology Transfer.' This is a strong indicator of the importance of transferring information to companies. NASA/ RECON is a good source for finding out what other companies are doing in the way of research. The Frequency Command (not available on the Aerospace Database) enables one to look at a breakdown of company research by NASA Thesaurus terms and quickly determine the interests of a set or a corporate source. NASA policy permits online access to all government agencies and contractors whose scientific and engineering activities are related to aeronautics and space research, and to universities or other organizations with aerospace-related grants, contracts or programs of interest to NASA.

Services to Small Business

NASA is interested in providing information to small and disadvantaged business firms through a special NASA Office of Small and Disadvantaged Business Utilization. This office publishes a very popular and useful document entitled *Selling to NASA*, an attractive and useful handbook for companies wishing to do business with NASA. Although most NASA contracts are for technical research and development, many contracts are of a nontechnical nature and provide opportunities for bidders. Another document of interest to potential NASA contractors is *How to Seek and Win NASA Contracts*, a compact and handy guide to the subject.

NASA TECH BRIEFS AND SPINOFF

Two of the most popular NASA publications aimed at businesses and other users are *NASA Tech Briefs* and *Spinoff*. Both of these attractive and readable publications are produced by NASA's Technology Utilization Division. They are aimed at telling different parts of NASA's 'technology transfer' story. *Spinoff* is an annual publication that has been published since 1976 and has a current press run of 75,000. Each year it colorfully presents how some

NASA-developed technology has been used by the the private sector during the previous year.

NASA Tech Briefs is prepared under the sponsorship of the National Aeronautics and Space Administration and published by Associated Business Publications twelve times a year. It includes drawings and descriptions of NASA developed technical advances. This useful publication is available to engineers, scientists, and information specialists at no charge. Since 1963, more than 13,000 *NASA Tech Briefs* issues have been made searchable on NASA/ RECON. Annual indexes are prepared by the NASA Scientific and Technical Information Facility using NASA Thesaurus terms. The publication is distributed free to approximately 160,000 recipients and contains 700 to 800 technical advances each year. Backing up *NASA Tech Briefs* are *Technical Support Packages* (TSP) that provide more detailed information on individual Tech Briefs. More than 100,000 requests are received each year for TSPs.

INDUSTRIAL APPLICATIONS CENTERS (IACs)

The NASA Technology Utilization Division (TU) also operates a number of application centers that provide a variety of online database systems, including NASA/RECON, to answer specific industry problems. This network includes ten Industrial Application Centers, thirty Industrial Application Affiliates, and ten Field Centers at NASA installations. Most states have a center waiting to serve the information needs of the business community. An example of one of these centers is the NERAC, Inc. formerly the New England Research Application Center in Tolland, Connecticut. which offers a wide variety of information services to businesses, from searching databases to published searches. Addresses for these centers may be found in any issue of *Spinoff* or *NASA Tech Briefs*.

TWO NASA SPECIAL PUBLICATIONS

Of the many NASA Special Publications, there are two in the Continuing Bibliographies series of special interest to businesses. These are *Management* and *NASA Patent Abstracts Bibliography*. The *Management* bibliography has been published annually since

1968 and includes citations from STAR and IAA. Indexed by NASA Thesaurus terms, it provides access to management informa- tion useful to NASA managers and administrators in science and technology.

The first section of *NASA Patent Abstracts Bibliography* includes the patents and patent illustrations for the most recent six-month's period. As the introduction states, it is published as a service to companies, firms, and individuals seeking new licensable products for the commercial market. The cumulative index, section 2, to the *NASA Patents Abstract Bibliography* indexes some 4,600 citations since May 1969 by NASA Thesaurus terms, inventor, corporate source, contract number, patent number, and accession number.

INDEX TO NEWS RELEASES AND SPEECHES

The *Index to NASA News Release and Speeches* is particularly valuable to business because of the speeches that are given by NASA Administrators to business groups. In this annual publica- tion, you can find indexed speeches filled with information vital to business. As an example, James Beggs presented a speech before the Business-Government Relations Council annual conference at Palm Beach, Florida in 1985 when he was still the NASA Adminis- trator. In this speech he describes instances of NASA's partnership with businesses:

> It has been estimated that in medicine alone, some 12,000 life-saving devices and processes owe their origins to aerospace research. These include programmable heart pacemakers and other programmable implantable systems that dispense medi-cation, alleviate pain and control blood pressure; surgical tools; and devices employed by paralyzed individuals in the pioneer field of computer-controlled walking.

AREOSPACE RESEARCH INFORMATION NETWORK (ARIN)

Often overlooked as a source of technology transfer information, ARIN is a goldmine of information about technology transfer and technology utilization. There are over 1,500 titles dealing with technology transfer topics. ARIN is an integrated library network serving the NASA family of libraries. The NASA libraries use ARIN to record both their current and retrospective titles. The ARIN system uses the NOTIS or Northwestern Online Total Integrated System software. Nearly one million records are available with nearly 300,000 held by NASA libraries and 700,000 other non-held records. This is a tremendous resource for technology transfer specialists and librarians alike.

TECHNOLOGY TRANSFER PARTNERSHIPS

The librarian's awareness of NASA's technology transfer programs enables librarians to be partners with the technology transfer specialists in the information enterprise of disseminating technology-rich information. Greater cooperation between these two groups is mutually beneficial and can enhance each other's information activity. Instead of focusing solely on NASA or a specific government agency technology transfer, librarians can broaden the sources of information of science and technology queries to include a greater range of resources and improved solutions.

Some of the more obvious technology transfer features of NASA's information programs have been presented here. For further information on any of the products mentioned in this article or in the bibliography contact the NASA Scientific and Technical Information Facility operated by RMS Associates, at P.O. Box 8757, BWI Airport, Maryland 21240.

BIBLIOGRAPHY

Buchan, Ronald L. & Phillip F. Eckert, Aerospace bibliographic control in Aeronautics and space flight collections (Special collections vol. 3 nos. 1/2, 1985/86) p.195-229.

Buchan, Ronald L., NASA/RECON its unique resources. *Sci-tech News*, August 1989, p. 86-88.

Buchan, Ronald L., The NASA STI Facility, *Sci-tech News*, October 1986, p.111-113.

COSMIC software catalog. 1990 edition. Supersedes all previous editions. Athens, GA: COSMIC; 440 p.

Cotter, Gladys. A., NASA scientific and technical information for the 1990's. *Government Information Quarterly*, symposium issue on NASA. Vol. 7, no. 2, 1990, p. 169-173.

Del Frate, Adelaide, NASA networks: The second time around. In *Sci-Tech Library Networks Within Organizations Science and Technology Libraries*, v. 8, No. 2, Winter 1987-88), p. 47-61.

Hawkins, Donald T. 'The Aerospace Database, In *Manual of Online Search Strategies*, edited by C.J. Armstrong & J.A. Large. Boston: G.K. Hall; 1987, p. 408-411.

How to seek and win NASA contracts, Washington: NASA; 1979, 29 p.

Index to NASA news releases and speeches. Washington: NASA; begun in 1967, annual since 1968. Coverage begins with 1963.

Jack, Robert F., The NASA/RECON search system; a file-by-file description of a major – but little known – collection of scientific information. *Online*, November 1982, Vol. 6, No. 6, p. 40-54.

Judson, Karen, Spinoffs from space. *USAir magazine*, February 20, 1990, p. 20-24.

Kavanagh, Stephen K. & Jay G. Miller, The Aerospace Database. *Database*. April 1986, p.61-67.

King, William R. & Gerald Zaltman, *Marketing scientific and technical information*. Boulder, Colo.: Westview Press; 1979, 247 p.

Management, a bibliography for NASA managers. Washington: NASA; annual 1968 to date, subtitle varies, NASA SP-7500.

Mogavero, Louis N. & Robert S. Shane, *Technology transfer and innovation*, (What every engineer should know about, a series). New York: Marcel Dekker; 1982, 154 p.

NASA Patent Abstracts Bibliography. Washington: NASA; (section 1, abstracts, section 2, cumulative index), semiannual, initial 1972 volume begins coverage with May 1969, NASA SP-7039.

NASA Tech Briefs. Washington: NASA; 1963 to date, frequency and format varies. Index to 1986 (etc.) NASA tech briefs. Washington: NASA; 1963 to date, frequency and title varies.

NASA Thesaurus. Washington: NASA; 3v., NASA SP-7064, 1988. & semi-annual NASA thesaurus supplement, 1989-.

Rose, Lester. Technology utilization: Managing the transfer of NASA aerospace technology to other industries. *Government information Quarterly*, symposium issue on NASA. vol. 7, no. 2, 1990, p. 175-183.

Selling to NASA, NASA Office of Small and Disadvantaged Business Utilization, Washington: NASA; 1986, 44 p.

Spinoff. Washington: NASA Office of Commercial Programs, Technology Utilization Division; annual, 1976 to date, (2nd year to date authored by James J. Haggerty).

The Role
of the Information Intermediary
in the Diffusion of Aerospace Knowledge

Thomas E. Pinelli
John M. Kennedy
Rebecca O. Barclay

SUMMARY. With its contribution to trade, its coupling with national security, and its symbolism, of U.S. technological strength, the U.S. aerospace industry holds a unique position in the nation's industrial structure. However, the U.S. aerospace industry is experiencing profound changes created by a combination of domestic actions and circumstances such as airline deregulation. Other changes result from external trends such as emerging foreign competition. These circumstances intensify the need to understand the production, tranfer, and utilization of knowledge as a precursor to the rapid diffusion of technology. This article presents a conceptual framework for understanding the diffusion of aerospace knowledge. The framework focuses on the information channels and members of the social system associated with the aerospace knowledge diffusion process, placing particular emphasis on aerospace librarians as information intermediaries.

Thomas E. Pinelli is Assistant to the Chief, Research Information and Applications Division, at the NASA Langley Research Center in Hampton, VA. He is a candidate for a PhD in Library and Information Science at Indiana University. John M. Kennedy is Director of the Center for Survey Research, Indiana University, Bloomington, IN. He is Principal Investigator of the NASA/DOD Aerospace Knowledge Diffusion Research Project. Rebecca O. Barclay is Faculty Member of the English Department at Old Dominion University in Norfolk, VA. She is also a doctoral student in Language, Linguistics, and Communication at Rensselaer Polytechnic Institute in Troy, NY.

59

INTRODUCTION

The ability of aerospace engineers and scientists to identify, acquire, and utilize scientific and technical information (STI) is of paramount importance to the efficiency of the research and development (R&D) process. Testimony to the central role of STI in the R&D process is found in numerous studies.[14] These studies show, among other things, that aerospace engineers and scientists devote more time, on the average, to the communication of technical information than to any other scientific or technical activity.[27] A number of studies have found strong relationships between the communication of STI and technical performance at both the individual[3,19,30] and the group level.[11,31,33] Therefore, we concur with Fisher's[14] conclusion that the "role of scientific and technical communication is thus central to the success of the innovation process, in general, and the management of R&D activities, in particular."

In terms of empirically derived data, very little is known about the diffusion of knowledge in the aerospace industry both in terms of the channels used to communicate the ideas and the information-gathering habits and practices of the members of the social system (i.e., aerospace engineers and scientists). Most of the channel studies, such as the work by Gilmore et al.,[17] and Archer,[5] have been concerned with the transfer of aerospace technology to non-aerospace industries.

Most of the studies involving aerospace engineers and scientists, such as the work by McCullough et al.,[24] and Monge et al.,[26] have been limited to the use of NASA STI products and services, and have not been concerned with information-gathering habits and practices. Although researchers such as Davis[12] and Spretnak[34] have investigated the importance of technical communications to engineers, it is not possible to determine from the published results if the study participants included aerospace engineers and scientists. It is likely that an understanding of the process by which aerospace knowledge is communicated through certain channels over time among the members of the social system would contribute to increasing productivity, stimulating innovation, and improving and maintaining the professional competence of U.S. aerospace engineers and scientists.

OVERVIEW OF THE FEDERAL AEROSPACE KNOWLEDGE DIFFUSION PROCESS

Figure 1 represents a model that depicts the transfer of federally funded aerospace R&D vis-à-vis the U.S. government technical report as being composed of two parts: the *informal* that relies on collegial contracts and the *formal* that relies on surrogates, information products, and information intermediaries to complete the "producer to user" transfer process. The producers are NASA and the DOD and their contractors and grantees. Producers depend upon surrogates and information intermediaries to complete the knowledge transfer process. When U.S. government technical reports are published, the initial or primary distribution is made to libraries and technical information centers. Copies are sent to surrogates for secondary and subsequent distribution. A limited number are set aside to be used by the author for the "scientist-to-scientist" exchange of information at the individual level.

Surrogates serve as technical report repositories or clearinghouses for the producers and include the Defense Technical Information Center (DTIC), the NASA Scientific and Technical Information Facility (NASA STIF), and the National Technical Information Service (NTIS). These surrogates have created a variety of technical report announcement journals such as TRAC (Tech-

FIGURE 1. A Model Depicting the Transfer of Federally Funded Aerospace R&D

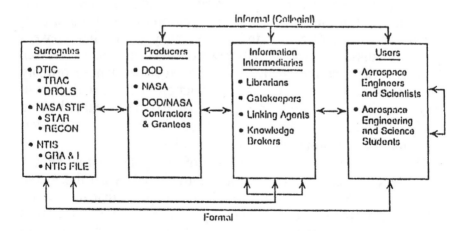

nical Report Announcement Circular) and STAR (Scientific and Technical Aerospace Reports) and computerized retrieval systems such as DROLS (Defense RDT&E On Line System) and RECON (REmote CONsole) that permit online access to technical report databases.

Information intermediaries are, in a large part, librarians and technical information specialists in academia, government, and industry. Those representing the producers serve as what McGowan and Loveless[25] describe as "knowledge brokers" or "linking agents." Information intermediaries connected with users act, according to Allen,[2] as "technological entrepreneurs" or "gatekeepers." The more "active" the intermediary, the more effective the transfer process becomes.[18] Active intermediaries take information from one place and move it to another, often face-to-face. Passive information intermediaries, on the other hand, "simply array information for the taking, relying on the initiative of the user to request or search out the information that may be needed."[13]

Problems With the Federal STI System

According to Ballard and his colleagues,[6] the problem with the total Federal STI system is "that the present system for transferring the results of federally-funded STI is passive, fragmented, and unfocused." Effective knowledge transfer is hindered by the fact that the Federal government "has no coherent or systematically designed approach to transferring the results of federally-funded R&D to the user."[6] In their study of issues and options in Federal STI, Bikson and her colleagues[8] found that many of the interviewees believed "dissemination activities were afterthoughts, undertaken without serious commitment by Federal agencies whose primary concerns were with [knowledge] production and not with knowledge transfer; [therefore,] much of what has been learned about [STI] and knowledge transfer has not been incorporated into federally-supported information transfer activities."

The problem with the *informal* part of the system is that knowledge users can learn from collegial contracts only what those contracts happen to know. Ample evidence supports that no one researcher can know about or keep up with all of the research in his/her area(s) of interest. Like other members of the scientific community, aerospace engineers and scientists are faced with the problem of too much information to know about, to keep up with, and to screen — information that is becoming more interdisciplinary in nature and more international in scope.

Two problems exist with the *formal* part of the system. First, the *formal* part of the system employs one-way source-to-user transmission. The problem with this kind of transmission is that such formal one-way "supply side" transfer procedures do not seem to be responsive to user context.[8] Rather, these efforts appear to start with an information system into which the users' requirements are retrofit.[1] The consensus of the findings from the empirical research is that interactive, two-way communications are required for effective information transfer.[8]

Second, the *formal* part relies heavily on information intermediaries to complete the knowledge transfer process. However, a strong methodological base for measuring or assessing the effectiveness of the information intermediary is lacking.[7] Empirical findings on the effectiveness of information intermediaries and the role(s) they play in knowledge transfer are sparse and inconclusive. In most studies, the value placed on and the use made of the information intermediary and information organization have been the criteria used in determining the intermediary's role in transferring the results of federally funded aerospace R&D. In addition, the impact of information intermediaries is likely to be strongly conditional and limited to a specific institutional context.

In a study conducted for the U.S. Department of Energy, King and his colleagues,[22] using a value added approach, investigated the contributions information intermediaries and organizations make to the value of information. First, they assume that information is a necessary commodity for conducting R&D. Second, they estimated that, were information unavailable from libraries/technical information centers, information substitutes would be more expensive and potentially less effective. Hypothetically, if information were not readily available, less actual information use would occur and less value would be derived from information seeking, thereby increasing the fundamental cost of R&D.

Federal policymakers may well ask if information intermediaries promote the effective transfer or diffusion of knowledge. Specific to this study, they may ask if information intermediaries promote the effective transfer or diffusion of federally funded aerospace R&D from producers to users. It is generally assumed that information intermediaries play a significant role in the knowledge diffusion process; however, their role in and contributions to the knowledge diffusion infrastructure are poorly understood.

Influence on Information-Seeking Behavior and Use

The nature of science and technology and the differences between engineers and scientists influence their information-seeking habits, practices, needs, and preferences and have significant implications for planning information services for these two groups.[35] Taylor,[36] quoting Brinberg[9] stresses that fundamental differences exist between engineers and scientists: "unlike scientists, the goal of the engineer is to produce or design a product, process, or system; not to publish and make original contributions to the literature. Engineers, unlike scientists, work within time constraints; they are not interested in theory, source data, and guides to literature nearly so much as they are in reliable answers to specific questions. Engineers prefer informal sources of information, especially conversations with individuals *within* their organization. Finally, engineers tend to minimize loss rather than maximize gain when seeking information."

Anthony et al.,[4] suggest that engineers may have psychological traits that predispose them to solving problems alone or with the help of colleagues rather than finding answers in the literature. They further state that "engineers like to solve their own problems. They draw on past experiences, use the trial and error method, and ask colleagues known to be efficient and reliable instead of searching or having someone search the literature for them. They are highly independent and self-reliant without being positively antisocial."

According to Allen,[2] "engineers read less than scientists, they use literature and libraries less, and seldom use information services which are directly oriented to them. They are more likely to use specific forms of literature such as handbooks, standards, specifications, and technical reports." What an engineer usually wants, according to Cairns and Compton,[10] "is a specific answer, in terms and format that are intelligible to him — not a collection of documents that he must sift, evaluate, and translate before he can apply them."

Young and Harriot[37] report that the "engineer's search for information seems to be more based on a need for specific problem solving than around a search for general opportunity. When they use the library it is more in a personal-search mode, generally not involving the professional (but nontechnical) librarian." Young and Harriot[37] conclude that "when engineers need technical information, they usually use the most accessible sources rather than searching for the highest quality sources. These accessible sources are respected colleagues, vendors, a familiar but possibly outdated text, and internal company [technical] report. He [the engineer] prefers informal information networks to the more formal search of publicly available and catalogued information."

Finally, engineers do tend to minimize loss rather than maximize gain when seeking information. Gerstberger and Allen,[16] in their study and choice of an information channel, note

> Engineers, in selecting among information channels, act in a manner which is intended not to maximize gain, but, rather to minimize loss. The loss to be minimized is the cost in terms of effort, either physical or psychological, which must be expended in order to gain access to an information channel.

Their behavior appears to follow a "law of least effort."[38] According to this law, individuals, when choosing among several paths to a goal, will base their decision upon the single criterion of "least average rate of probable work." According to Gerstberger and Allen,[16] engineers appear to be governed or influenced by a principle closely related to this law. They attempt to minimize effort in terms of work required to gain access to an information channel/source. Gerstberger and Allen[16] reached the following conclusions:

1. Accessibility is the single most important determinant of the overall extent to which an information channel/source is used by an engineer.
2. Both accessibility and perceived technical quality influence the choice of the first source.

3. Perception of accessibility is influenced by experience. The more experience engineers have with an information channel/ source, the more accessible they perceive it to be.

Rosenberg's[28] findings also support the conclusions by Gerstberger and Allen[16] that accessibility almost exclusively determines the frequency of use of information channels. Rosenberg[28] concluded that researchers minimize the cost of obtaining information while sacrificing the quality of the information received.

In his study of the *Factors Related to the Use of Technical Information in Engineering Problem Solving*, Kaufman[21] reported that the engineers in his study rated *technical quality* or *reliability* followed by *relevance* as the criteria used in choosing the most useful information source. However, *accessibility* appears to be the criteria used most often for choosing an information source *even if that source* proved to be the least useful.

Use of Libraries and Library Services

The process by which engineers solve technical problems affects their use of libraries and library services. The results of Shuchman's[32] study, which are supported by the findings of several engineering information use studies, confirm this position. The steps the engineers in Shuchman's[32] study followed in solving technical problems appear below.

HOW ENGINEERS SOLVE TECHNICAL PROBLEMS

Steps in Solving Technical Problems	*Percent of Cases*
1. Consulted personal store of technical information	93
2. Informal discussion with colleagues	87
3. Discussed problem with supervisor	61
4. Consulted internal technical reports	50
5. Consulted key person in firm who usually knows new information	38
6. Consulted library sources (e.g., technical journals, conference proceedings)	35

7. Consulted outside consultant	33
8. Used electronic databases	20
9. Consulted librarian/technical information specialist	14
10. No pattern in problem solving	5

Herner[20] found that engineers at Johns Hopkins University considered their personal knowledge and informal discussions with colleagues and with experts within their organization to be most useful when faced with solving a technical problem. Rosenbloom and Wolek[29] found that engineers favored the use of interpersonal communications (e.g., discussions with colleagues within their organization) when faced with the need to solve a technical problem. These findings are supported by Kremer[23] and Kaufman.[21] Only after they have exhausted their personal store of information and have consulted their colleagues do engineers turn to another information source, such as a library.

In Shuchman's study,[32] libraries ranked sixth in solving a technical problem. The fact that librarians and technical information specialists ranked ninth as the information source engineers used in solving a technical problem supports the hypothesis that engineers tend to assume personal responsibility for fulfilling their information needs. This statement is supported by Shuchman's finding that engineers in her study attempted to find the information themselves in the library before soliciting the help of a librarian or technical information specialist.

Allen[2] corroborated these findings, noting that although the library is an important source of information, rarely do engineers make full use of its potential. He too reported that engineers prefer to search for library information themselves, not only in "rare" instances seeking the services of a librarian or technical information specialist.

Other studies suggest several reasons why engineers do not seek technical information in libraries. Apart from engineers, "personal" and "informally" directed approach to fulfilling their information needs, Frohman,[12] quoted by Allen,[2] states that the extent of library use is related inversely to the distance separating the user from the library. Allen[2] summarized his discussion of library use by observing that "the value seen in using the library simply does not

seem great enough to overcome the effort involved in either travel-
ing to it or using it once the person is there."

Information on the use of electronic bibliographic databases by
engineers is limited. Those engineers who participated in Shuchman's[32] study made little use of the online databases. In steps used
in solving a technical problem, databases ranked eighth, just before
librarians and technical information specialists. Kaufman[21] found
that approximately five percent of the engineers in his study used
online databases when searching for a solution to a technical problem. Engineers in Kaufman's[21] study indicated that "accessibility"
was the single most important criterion for determining the use of
an online database. Furthermore, when the engineers in Kaufman's[21] study did use online databases, they did so most frequently
to define or redefine the technical problem and continued to use the
databases for the duration of the attempt to solve the technical problem.

As shown in the chart that follows, aerospace engineers and scientists use a variety of information sources when solving a technical
problem.[27] They use, in decreasing order of frequency, the following sources.

SOURCES USED
BY AEROSPACE ENGINEERS AND SCIENTISTS
TO SOLVE TECHNICAL PROBLEMS

Sources	Percentage of Cases
1. Personal Knowledge	88.7
2. Informal discussion with colleagues	77.2
3. Discussions with experts within the organization	69.5
4. Discussion with supervisor	45.1
5. Textbooks	39.6
6. Technical reports	35.4
7. Journals and conference/meeting papers	35.2
8. Handbooks and standards	34.5
9. Goverment technical reports	33.5

10. Discussions with experts outside of
    the organization   25.5
11. Librarians/technical information
    specialists   14.1
12. Technical information sources such as
    online databases   8.2

In an attempt to validate the findings, the sources used by the aerospace engineers[27] were compared with the steps used by the engineers in Shuchman's[32] study of *Information Transfer in Engineering*. With minor exceptions, the aerospace engineers and scientists sought information from sources similar to the sources used by engineers in Shuchman's[32] study. Both groups begin with what Allen[2] calls an "informal search for information followed by the use of formal information sources." Having completed these steps, engineers turn to librarians and library services for assistance.

NASA/DOD AEROSPACE KNOWLEDGE DIFFUSION RESEARCH PROJECT

The *NASA/DOD Aerospace Knowledge Diffusion Research Project* is a cooperative effort that is sponsored by NASA, Office of Aeronautics, Exploration and Technology (OAET) and the DOD, Office of the Assistant Secretary of the Air Force, Deputy for Scientific and Technical Information. The research project is a joint effort of the Indiana University, Center for Survey Research, and the NASA Langley Research Center. As scholarly inquiry, the project has both an immediate and long term purpose. In the first instance, it provides a practical and pragmatic basis for understanding how the results of NASA/DOD research diffuse into the aerospace R&D process. Over the long term, it will provide an empirical basis for understanding the aerospace knowledge diffusion process itself and its implications at the individual, organizational, national, and international levels.

Despite the vast amount of scientific and technical information (STI) available to potential users, several major barriers to effective knowledge diffusion exist. First, the very low level support for knowledge transfer in comparison to knowledge production suggests that dissemination efforts are not viewed as an important component of the R&D process. Second, there are mounting reports from users about difficulties in getting appropriate information in forms useful for problem solving and decision making. Third, rapid advances in many areas of S&T knowledge can be fully exploited only if they are quickly translated into further research and application. Although the United States dominates basic R&D, foreign competitors may be better able to apply the results. Fourth, current mechanisms are often inadequate to help the user assess the quality of available information. Fifth, the characteristics of actual usage behavior are not sufficiently taken into account in making available useful and easily retrieved information.

These deficiencies must be remedied if the results of NASA/DOD funded R&D are to be successfully applied to innovation, problem solving, and productivity. Only by maximizing the R&D process can the United States maintain its international competitive edge in aerospace. The *NASA/DOD Aerospace Knowledge Diffusion Research Project* will provide descriptive and analytical data regarding the flow of STI at the individual, organizational, national, and international levels. It will examine both the channels used to communicate information and the social system of the aerospace knowledge diffusion process. The results of the project should provide useful information to R&D managers, information managers, and others concerned with improving access to and utilization of STI.

Project Assumption

1. Rapid diffusion of technology and technological developments requires an understanding of the aerospace knowledge diffusion process.
2. Knowledge production, transfer, and utilization are equally important components of the aerospace knowledge diffusion process.
3. Understanding the channels; the information products involved the production, transfer, and utilization of aerospace information; and the information-seeking habits, practices,

and preferences of aerospace engineers and scientists is necessary to understanding aerospace knowledge diffusion.

4. The knowledge derived from federally funded aerospace R&D is indispensable in maintaining the vitality and international competitiveness of the U.S. aerospace industry and essential to maintaining and improving the professional competency of U.S. aerospace engineers and scientists.

5. The U.S. government technical report plays an important, but as yet undefined, role in the transfer and utilization of knowledge derived from federally funded aerospace R&D.

6. Librarians, as information intermediaries, play an important, but as yet undefined, role in the transfer and utilization of knowledge derived from federally funded aerospace R&D.

Project Objectives

1. Understanding the aerospace knowledge diffusion process at the individual, organizational, and national levels, placing particular emphasis on the diffusion of federally funded aerospace STI.

2. Understanding the international aerospace knowledge diffusion process at the individual and organizational levels, placing particular emphasis on the systems used to diffuse the results of government funded aerospace R&D.

3. Understanding the roles played by the NASA/DOD technical reports and aerospace librarians in the transfer and utilization of knowledge derived from federally funded aerospace R&D.

4. Achieving recognition and acceptance within NASA and the DOD and throughout the aerospace community that STI is a valuable strategic source for innovation, problem solving, and productivity.

5. Providing results that can be used to optimize the effectiveness and efficiency of the Federal STI aerospace transfer system and exchange mechanism.

The Role of Aerospace Librarians
in Knowledge Transfer

How do librarians as information intermediaries promote/facili-
tate the transfer of federally funded aerospace knowledge? Several
approaches will be used to make this determination. In *Phase 1* a
random sample of U.S. aerospace engineers and scientists who are
members of the American Institute of Aeronautics and Astronautics
(AIAA) were surveyed to determine their information-seeking
habits and preferences. The questionnaires sent to the sample covered a range of information-seeking and use activities including use
of aerospace libraries and library services. The questions covered
such factors as relative use and importance of the library, distance
from the user, reasons for not using the library, use of electronic
databases, and the use of library in problem solving.

Phase 2 includes a survey of approximately 325 U.S. aerospace
libraries in government and industry. Questionnaires covered a variety of topics such as NASA/DOD technical reports, use of print
and online databases, use of information technology, marketing
strategies, services provided, and a variety of questions concerning
the role of information intermediaries in knowledge transfer. *Phase
3* includes a survey of approximately 70 U.S. academic aerospace/
engineering libraries. Topics covered were similar to those covered
in *Phase 2*. In addition, aerospace faculty and undergraduate students were also surveyed to determine their information-seeking
habits and practices. Faculty and students were asked a number of
questions regarding their use of libraries and library services. *Phase
4* involves a survey of non-U.S. aerospace engineers and scientists,
information intermediaries, faculty and students. Topics covered
are similar to those covered in *Phases 1, 2, and 3*. The non-U.S.
data will permit the comparison of systems to determine similarities
and differences. Having completed these phases, we can begin to
develop an empirical basis for understanding the aerospace knowledge diffusion process itself; the implications at the individual, organizational, national, and international levels; and the role that the
information intermediary plays in the transfer of federally funded
aerospace STI.

CONCLUDING REMARKS

Although the U.S. aerospace industry continues to be the leading positive contributor to the balance of trade among all merchandise industries, it is experiencing significant changes whose implications may not be well understood.* Increasing U.S. collaboration with foreign producers will result in a more international manufacturing environment, altering the current structure of the aerospace industry. International alliances will result in a more rapid diffusion of technology, increasing pressure on U.S. aerospace companies to push forward with new technological developments and to take steps designed to maximize the inclusion of recent technological developments into the R&D process.

To remain a world leader in aerospace, the U.S. must take the steps necessary to improve and maintain the profession competency of U.S. aerospace engineers and scientists and to enhance innovation and productivity as well as to maximize the inclusion of recent technological developments into the R&D process. How well these objectives are met, and at what cost depends on a variety of factors, but largely on the ability of U.S. aerospace engineers and scientists to acquire and process the results of NASA/DOD funded aerospace R&D. Furthermore, it is likely that an understanding of the process by which STI in aerospace industry is communicated through certain channels over time among the members of the social system will contribute to increasing productivity, stimulating innovation and improving and maintaining the professional competence of U.S. aerospace engineers and scientists.

The knowledge diffusion process is complex. A myriad of factors influence the conception, initiation, and operation of the process. A wide range of commonly recognized elements and influences are implicit in the process. Even if all the practical and theoretical elements of the knowledge diffusion process were understood, the success of the "diffusion" of knowledge would not necessarily be assured. One determinant of success is the presence of an "active"

---

*"Aerospace" includes aeronautics, space science, space technology, and related fields.

knowledge diffusion mechanism which involves the participation of "linking agents" who can assist the potential knowledge user in identifying information requirements/needs, identify knowledge that can meet those needs, and indirectly promote communication between the knowledge producers and users. Defining the role that information intermediaries play in the transfer and utilization of aerospace R&D may contribute to increased effectiveness and efficiency in the Federal STI aerospace knowledge transfer system and exchange mechanism.

REFERENCES

1. Adam, Ralph. "Pulling the Minds of Social Scientists Together: Towards a World Social Science Information System." *International Social Science Journal* 27:3 (1975): 519-531.

2. Allen, Thomas J. *Managing the Flow of Technology: Technology Transfer and the Dissemination of Technological Information Within the R&D Organization.* (Cambridge, MA: MIT Press, 1977.)

3. Allen, Thomas J. "Roles in Technical Communication Networks." In *Communication Among Scientists and Engineers*, Carnot E. Nelson and Donald K. Pollack, eds. (Lexington, MA: D.C. Heath, 1970) 191-208.

4. Anthony L.J.; H. East; and M.J. Slater. "The Growth of Literature of Physics." *Reports on Progress in Physics* 32 (1969): 709-767.

5. Archer, John F. *The Diffusion of Space Technology By Means of Technical Publications: A Report Based on the Distribution, Use, and Effectiveness of "Selected Welding Techniques."* Boston: American Academy of Arts and Sciences, November 1964. (Available from NTIS Springfield, VA; 70N76955.)

6. Ballard, Steve et al., *Improving the Transfer and Use of Scientific and Technical Information. The Federal Role: Volume 2—Problems and Issues in the Transfer and Use of STI.* Washington, DC: National Science Foundation, 1986. (Available from NTIS, Springfield, VA PB-87-142923.)

7. Beyer, Janice M. and Harrison M. Trice. "The Utilization Process: A Conceptual Framework and Synthesis of Empirical Findings." *Administrative Science Quarterly* 27 (December 1982): 591-622.

8. Bikson, Tora K.; Barbara E. Quint; and Leland L. Johnson. *Scientific and Technical Information Transfer: Issues and Options*. Washington, DC: National Science Foundation, March 1984. (Available from NTIS, Springfield, VA PB-85-150357; also available as Rand Note 2131.)

9. Brinberg, Herbert R. "The Contribution of Information to Economic Growth and Development." Paper presented at 40th Congress of the International Federation for Documentation. Copenhagen, Denmark. August 1980.

10. Cairns, R.W. and Bertita E. Compton. "The SATCOM Report and the

Engineer's Information Problem." *Engineering Education* 60:5 (January 1970): 375-376.

11. Carter, C.F. and B.R. Williams. *Industry and Technical Progress: Factors Governing the Speed of Application of Science.* (London: Oxford University Press, 1957).

12. Davis, Richard M. "How Important is Technical Writing? — A Survey of the Opinions of Successful Engineers." *Technical Writing Teacher* 4:3 (Spring 1977): 83-88.

13. Eveland, J.D. *Scientific and Technical Information Exchange Issues and Findings.* Washington, DC: National Science Foundation, March 1987. (Not available from NTIS.)

14. Fischer, William A. "Scientific and Technical Information and the Performance of R&D Groups." in *Management of Research and Innovation.* Burton V. Dean and Joel L. Goldhar, eds. (NY: North-Holland Publishing Company, 1980), 67-89.

15. Frohman, A. *Polaroid Library Usage Study.* Cambridge, MA: M.I.T. Sloan School of Management, 1968, Term Paper.

16. Gerstberger, Peter G. and Thomas J. Allen. "Criteria Used by Research and Development Engineers in the Selection of an Information Source," *Journal of Applied Psychology* 52:4 (August 1968): 272-279.

17. Gilmore, John S. et al., *The Channels of Technology Acquisition in Commercial Firms and the NASA Dissemination Program.* Denver, CO: Denver Research Institute, June 1967. (Available from: NTIS Springfield, VA; N67-31477.)

18. Goldhor, Richard S. and Robert T. Lund. "University-to-Industry Advanced Technology Transfer: A Case Study." *Research Policy* 12 (1983): 121-152.

19. Hall, K.R. and E. Ritchie. "A Study of Communication Behavior in an R&D Laboratory." *R&D Management* 5 (1975): 243-245.

20. Herner, Saul. "Information Gathering Habits of Workers in Pure and Applied Science." *Industrial and Engineering Chemistry* 46:1 (January 1954): 228-236.

21. Kaufman, Harold G. *Factors Related to Use of Technical Information in Engineering Problem Solving.* Brooklyn, NY: Polytechnic Institute of New York, 1983.

22. King, Donald W., Jose-Maire Griffiths, Ellen A. Sweet, and Robert R.V. Wiederkehr. *A Study of the Value of Information and the Effect on Value of Intermediary Organizations, Timeliness of Services and Products, and Comprehensiveness of EDB.* Rockville, MD: King Research, 1984. (Available from NTIS, Springfield, VA DE82014250).

23. Kremer, Jeanette M. *Information Flow Among Engineers in a Design Company.* Ph.D. Diss., University of Illinois at Urbana-Champaign, 1980. UMI, 1980. 80-17965.

24. McCullough, Robert A. et al. *A Review and Evaluation of the Langley Research Center's Scientific and Technical Information Program. Results of*

Phase VI. The Technical Report: A Survey and Analysis. Washington, DC: National Aeronautics and Space Administration. NASA TM-83269. April 1982. (Available from NTIS, Springfield, VA; 87N70843.)

25. McGowan, Robert P. and Stephen Loveless. "Strategies for Information Management: The Administrator's Perspective." *Public Administrative Review* 41:3 (May/June 1981): 331-339.

26. Monge, Peter R., James D. Schriner, Bettie F. Farace, and Richard V. Farace. *The Assessment of NASA Technical Information*. NASA CR-181367. East Lansing, MI: Communimetrics, October 1979. (Available from NTIS, Springfield, VA; 87N70893).

27. Pinelli, Thomas E., Myron Glassman, Walter E. Olui, and Rebecca O. Barclay. *Technical Communications in Aeronautics: Results of an Exploratory Study*. Washington, DC: National Aeronautics and Space Administration. NASA TM-101534, Part I, February 1989. (Available from NTIS, Springfield, VA: 89N26772).

28. Rosenberg, Victor. "Factors Affecting the Preferences of Industrial Personnel for Information Gathering Methods." *Information Storage and Retrieval* 3 (July 1967): 119-127.

29. Rosenbloom, Richard S. and Francis W. Woleck. *Technology and Information Transfer: A Survey of Practice in Industrial Organizations*. (Boston: Harvard University, 1970).

30. Rothwell, R. and A.B. Robertson. "The Role of Communications in Technological Innovation." *Research Policy* 2 (1973): 204-225.

31. Rubenstein, A.H., R.T. Barth, and C.F. Douds. "Ways to Improve Communications Between R&D Groups." *Research Management* (November 1971): 49-59.

32. Shuchman, Hedvah L. *Information Transfer in Engineering*. (Glastonbury, CT: The Futures Group, 1981).

33. Smith, C.G. "Consultation and Decision Processes in a Research and Development Laboratory." *Administrative Science Quarterly* 15 (1970): 203-215.

34. Spretnak, Charlene M. "A Survey of the Frequency and Importance of Technical Communication in an Engineering Career," *Technical Writing Teacher* 9:3 (Spring 1972): 133-136.

35. System Development Corporation. *A System Study of Abstracting and Indexing in the United States*. Technical Memorandum WD-394. Falls Church, VA: System Development Corporation, 16 December 1966. (Available from NTIS, Springfield, VA; PB 174 249.)

36. Taylor, Robert S. *Value-Added Processes in Information Systems*. (Norwood, NJ: Ablex Press, 1986).

37. Young, J.F. and L.C. Harriott. "The Changing Technical Life of Engineers." *Mechanical Engineering* 101:1 (January 1979): 20-24.

38. Zipf, Geo K. *Human Behavior and the Principle of Least Effort*. (Cambridge, MA: Addison-Wesley, 1949).

The Role of Libraries
in Technology Transfer
for Agriculture

Kathleen C. Hayes

SUMMARY. This paper examines the economic situation of the
Nation and agriculture's use of technology transfer to improve its
competitiveness in the global marketplace. Information is viewed as
an economic resource and thus the roles of libraries and information
professionals are perceived to be important to the technology transfer process. The National Agricultural Library, U.S. Department of
Agriculture, is examining its Federal role in technology transfer and
examples of its activities are discussed.

INTRODUCTION

The twentieth century witnessed the blossoming of American enterprise. The foundations of that evolution were abundant resources, a vast and inexpensive labor supply generated by agricultural efficiencies and waves of immigrants, and a national
infrastructure of science-based research at Federal laboratories and
state universities.

Kathleen C. Hayes is Coordinator of the Technology Transfer Information
Center for the National Agricultural Library, Beltsville, MD. Ms. Hayes has
worked as Information Specialist for five years and recently returned from an
assignment with the Joint Council on Food and Agricultural Sciences. She previously was employed by the Cooperative Extension Service, The Pennsylvania
State University. Ms. Hayes holds a BS in Home Economics and a MS in Agriculture and Extension Education.

The opinions in this article represent those of the author and do not necessarily
reflect those of the National Agricultural Library or the U.S. Department of Agriculture.

However, as the 21st century approaches the United States is in a far different economic situation. The forces driving the economy are: intense global competition; new patterns of capital formation; growing entrepreneurship; rapid technological advances fueling new enterprises; and changing demographics.

This situation is not limited solely to the United States. It is shaking the economic and political foundations of Western and Eastern Europe, and the Soviet Union. It also is transforming the economies of North and South America, and the nations and city-states of the Pacific Rim.

Many agree that the successful economy of the future will be closely indexed to technology. The creation of technology is important, but perhaps even more important is the ability to convert that technology rapidly into commercial products that meet the needs of society.

TECHNOLOGY TRANSFER LEGISLATION

The United States invests heavily in technology, which is defined as the "utilization of both scientific and technical resources." These Federal investments help the United States maintain its position as the leader in creativity and innovation. Scientists and engineers in Federal and university laboratories are assets to the Nation as they generate important advances and new technologies.

Technology transfer legislation is a means to effectively capitalize on these ideas and innovations, and transform them into products that can be sold in the world marketplace.

The Technology Transfer Act of 1986 (P.L. 99502) amends the original legislation, the Stevenson Wydler Act of 1980 (P.L. 96-480) and authorizes Federal-Industrial Cooperative Research and Development Agreements (CRDAs) which permit:

— Federal laboratories and staff to work with individual firms, nonprofits organizations, and others. The emphasis is on small businesses.

— Federal research laboratories to "accept, retain, and use funds, personnel, services, and property from collaborating parties and also to provide personnel, services, and property to collaborating parties.''

— Up-front patent licensing and royalty agreements, and

— 15 percent of the royalties collected under such agreement (or any other patent license) to be paid to Federal scientists named on the patents as inventors (up to $100,000 per inventor per year).

The remainder of the royalties can be used:

— To pay the direct expenses of administering the patent licensing program.

— To reward other scientists and support personnel who contributed to the research question, and

— For other activities that enhance related ongoing research. The maximum royalties that can be retained by a Federal research entity is 5 percent of its total R&D budget.

AGRICULTURE FACES WORLDWIDE COMPETITION

U.S. agriculture is the world's largest commercial industry with assets of approximately $1.4 trillion.[1] Agriculture accounts for 17 percent of the gross national product and employs more than 20 million people.[2] The continued effective production, marketing, processing, and distribution of the Nation's agricultural abundance are of significant social, economic, and political importance.

As agriculture enters the decade of the 1990s, it is faced with the same intense global competition as many other sectors of the economy. Agriculture relies heavily on exports, and the dramatic changes taking place around the globe require a more assertive approach. Knowledge of demographic, social, cultural, economic, and policy factors that influence the demand for U.S. products in world markets must be used to develop new markets and new products that are in demand, and also to add value to existing products to make them available in the form and quality desired by the world community.

U.S. DEPARTMENT OF AGRICULTURE'S ROLE IN TECHNOLOGY TRANSFER

For more than a century, agriculture has relied on the extension education concept of using county-based personnel to get the research results from the federal laboratories and state land-grant universities into the hands of producers and agribusinesses throughout the Nation. The transfer of the research-based knowledge and technologies, and the implementation of them by agricultural producers have contributed to the success of the agricultural industry.

This system of cooperation is still in place and its guardians are aware of the need to work together to reach the goal of economic competitiveness. Examples of recent accomplishments and current activities directed toward competitiveness include:

— Research and development programs that resulted in the commercialization of new products made from contemporary agricultural commodities such as starch-based plastics, printer's ink from soybeans, and a no-calorie, high-fiber flour extender from cereal grain hulls and corn cobs.

— Diversification programs that resulted in native pecan groves becoming commercial orchards, catfish and tilapia being raised by livestock producers, and the raising of exotic wildlife for meat or for sport hunting.

— Demonstration projects that are using industrial raw materials from agriculture such as: kenaf for newsprint, guayule for natural rubber, and crambe/rapeseed for lubricating oils and plastics.

In 1989 personnel from 13 Federal agencies within USDA cooperated to produce a publication entitled *Technology Transfer: A Profile of Agency Activities in USDA*. The publication contains a description of each agency's mission and responsibilities, its role in technology transfer and examples of successful transfers to the private sector. The publication also identifies the types of technologies required by the agencies and should be helpful to entrepreneurs who are seeking technical assistance from or looking to market a new product to the Federal government.

NATIONAL AGRICULTURAL LIBRARY'S ROLE
IN TECHNOLOGY TRANSFER

The mission of the National Agricultural Library (NAL) is ". . . to acquire and to diffuse among the people of the United States useful information on subjects connected with agriculture in the most general and comprehensive sense of that word."

Consider the challenge of organizing and managing data at a time when libraries are undergoing a technological evolution and also during an era known as the Information Age. Add to this dilemma the multidisciplinary needs of the Nation's food and fiber system that is faced with intense competition in the global marketplace. Further contemplate the scientific and technological breakthroughs such as biotechnology, the challenges of global climate change, and the overall necessity to produce economically viable products in an environmentally sound manner.

Place all of this within the framework of "information as an economic resource" as described in the Glenerin Declaration.[3]

> We have moved from an industrial to an information age, where the efficient exploitation of information as an economic resource and a sector of production has become crucial to the achievement of economic growth. In the countries of Canada, the United Kingdom, and the United States the production, distribution and use of information have become matters of strategic economic, social and political importance. To ensure that the benefits of the information age are fully realized, it is necessary to create and maintain an environment which provides for the open and unrestricted exchange of information. Such open access, though must be consistent with the protection of individual rights, appropriate economic incentives, and the sovereignty concerns of nation-states as determined by their unique circumstances.[4]

When all of these circumstances are considered, the roles of libraries, librarians, and information specialists are significant to the technology transfer process. Libraries are sources of printed and unprinted information. Librarians and other information professionals are trained to ask the right questions and also to seek answers through reference materials, such as encyclopedias, indexes, databases, and human resources. Also, information professionals benefit from an interlibrary network for locating and/or lending resources that has been in place for years.

The sophisticated national and international information infrastructure that exists through library networks continues to improve as new electronic technologies and information systems are developed and utilized. This infrastructure enhances the ability to locate and access information around the world.

Librarians and other professionals who serve as information brokers may need to recognize that they have the opportunity to provide what is potentially the "missing link" of data to a scientist, educator, student, or entrepreneur who may be on the "brink of discovery." To that extent, information is an economic resource, and the technology transfer concept of excellence as a work ethic is critical. Librarians and information specialists can assist in the technology transfer process and ultimately the Nation's economic competitiveness by understanding the subject matter and also comprehending the importance of connecting the client to the correct information in a timely manner.

Technology transfer has been an NAL initiative since January 1988. The National Agricultural Library has both a challenge and an opportunity to further examine and expand its Federal role, and the roles of libraries and librarians in the technology transfer process. A sampling of NAL's technology transfer activities follow.

Technology Transfer Information Center. In December 1989 NAL established a Technology Transfer Information Center to provide enhanced services to current clientele and also to develop new service relationships with representatives from other Federal agencies and laboratories, the Federal Laboratory Consortium, university technology centers and centers of excellence, libraries, public interest groups, associations, and the private sector.

The Technology Transfer Information Center has a coordinator who is responsible for developing a national technology transfer information system that provides information and referral services; enhances the collection of books, journals, and other resources; develops information products; coordinates outreach activities; and establishes dissemination networks.

Collection Development. Rapid access to current information is critical to scientists and educators as they strive to improve agricultural productivity and competitiveness. In addition to the traditional scientific literature that NAL collects, the Library is purchasing and processing publications that focus on leadership, strategic planning, critical thinking, innovation, creativity, entrepreneurship, home-based and small business management, venture capital, patents, and licensing agreements.

Information Delivery Systems. The Library's electronic, bibliographic database, AGRICOLA, assures timely, cost-effective access to literature. AGRICOLA is available as an online database and also on CD-ROM.

Technology specialists at NAL are experimenting with capturing full-text, including images, in digital format for publication on CD-ROM disks. This type of integrated digital information management system offers word-searchable text as well as the possibility of electronic delivery of publications to remote sites via telecommunication networks.

Technical Consultation. These technology specialists and other NAL professionals are conducting applied research on technologies, such as an electronic bulletin board and expert advisory and hypermedia systems, to determine if and how the technologies can assist the agency to achieve its mission of preserving, managing, and/or disseminating information. As the early adopters of information technologies, NAL staff are available to provide technical assistance to both the public and the private sectors.

Outreach. In 1988 NAL sponsored a forum to discuss and disseminate information on the practical application of new technologies within the library and information communities. Proceedings from this conference entitled *Application of Scanning Methodologies in Libraries* are available to the private sector. The Library also held an open house in 1989 to display and discuss information management-related entrepreneurial opportunities with the private sector.

CONCLUSION

Experts across the country claim that technology transfer is a "contact sport." It requires: people to people contact; the establishment of networks throughout the Federal laboratory, state university, and national library network systems; diligence in locating data; and a passionate belief that the "T-squared" process can work to enhance the competitiveness of the United States in the global marketplace. It is obvious that there are both challenges and opportunities for NAL to participate in the process of technology transfer.

FIGURE 1. New Logo of the Library's Technology Transfer Information Center

PHOTO 1: Fiber rich baked goods held by J. Michael Gould, chemist at the Agricultural Research Service (ARS) Northern Regional Research Center in Peoria, IL, are made from a no-calorie, high-fiber flour, based on a process he invented with biologist Lee Dexter to soften fibrous parts of cereal crops so they can be ground up and used as flour. The patented process, one of 418 patents granted to ARS in the past ten years, has been licensed to commercial firms which will produce the dietary fiber from oat hulls, corn cobs, etc. to sell to bakeries to enrich the fiber contents of regular flours while reducing the calories of baked products.

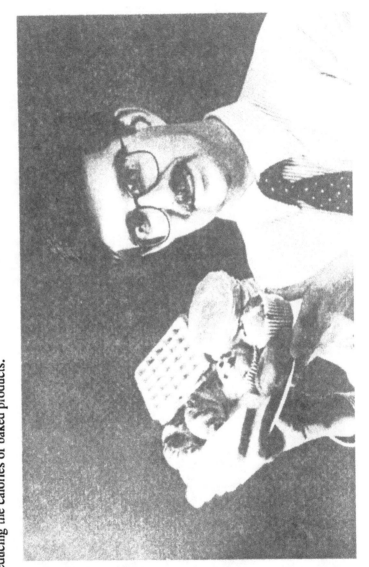

PHOTO 2: Felix Otey, a chemist with the Agricultural Research Service in Peoria, IL, holds a sheet of biodegradable plastic film that he helped to develop. The commercially produced film is made from corn starch and petroleum-based poly-

ENDNOTES

1. Joint Council on Food and Agricultural Sciences. *Fiscal Year 1991 Priorities for Research, Extension, and Higher Education: A Report to the Secretary of Agriculture*; 1989 June. p. 1.
2. U.S. Government Accounting Office. *Government Accounting Office Report to the Secretary of Agriculture: U.S. Department of Agriculture Interim Report on Ways to Enhance Management*; 1989 October. p. 3.
3. U.S. National Commission of Libraries and Information Science. *Annual Report on National Commission of Libraries and Information Science, 1987-1988*; p. 42.
4. Ibid.

REFERENCES

CORETECH. *National Research and Development Policies for 1988 and Beyond: The CORETECH Agenda*. Washington, DC: Council on Research and Technology; n.d. 33 p.

Frank, Robyn C. NAL's Information Center Approach, *Agricultural Libraries Information Notes*, 14 (1/2); 1988.

Gerwitz, Adina R. A New World of Knowledge: College Park's Libraries Face the Demands and Opportunities of an Information Age. *College Park: University of Maryland Alumni Magazine*, 1 (2): 9-13; 1990 Spring.

Hayes, Kathleen C. Technology Transfer and the National Agricultural Library. *Agricultural Libraries Information Notes*, 15 (11/12): 1-3; 1989.

Hayes, Kathleen C.; Maher Theodore J.; and Hall James T. *Technology Transfer: A Profile of Agency Activities in USDA*. Washington, DC: U.S. Department of Agriculture, Research and Education Committee, Technology Transfer Subcommittee; 1989 March. 38 p.

Joint Council on Food and Agricultural Sciences. *Fiscal Year 1991 Priorities for Research, Extension, and Higher Education: A Report to the Secretary of Agriculture*. Washington, DC: Joint Council on Food and Agricultural Sciences; 1989 June. 50 p.

Joint Council on Food and Agricultural Sciences. *Fiscal year 1992 Priorities for Research, Extension, and Higher Education: A Report to the Secretary of Agriculture*. Washington, DC: Joint Council on Food and Agricultural Sciences; 1990 June.

McNeal, C. David et al. Alternative Agricultural Opportunities. *1989 Accomplishments Report for Research, Extension, and Higher Education: A Report to the Secretary of Agriculture*. Washington, DC: Joint Council on Food and Agricultural Sciences; 1989 November; p. 5-7.

Tatsuno, Sheridan. The Technopolis Strategy: Implications for the United States. In: *Managing the Knowledge Asset into the 21st Century: Focus on Research Consortia*. Cambridge, MA: Technology Strategy Group; 1988; p. 33-40.

U.S. Department of Agriculture. *The Mission of the National Agricultural Library.* n.p. 1981 October. 11 p.

U.S. Government Accounting Office. *Government Accounting Office Report to the Secretary of Agriculture: U.S. Department of Agriculture Interim Report on Ways to Enhance Management.* Washington, DC: U.S. Government Accounting Office; 1989 October. 67 p.

U.S. National Commission of Libraries and Information Science. *Annual Report on National Commission of Libraries and Information Science, 1987-1988.* Washington, DC: U.S. National Commission of Libraries and Information Science; 1989 April. 48 p.

The Public Library:
A Key to Technology Transfer

Cheryl Engel

Public libraries promote technology transfer by acting as important centers for information transfer. Free to all, the public library provides an ideal regional access point for individuals, corporations and local governments seeking information on new technologies. Using the Science and Technology Department of the Carnegie Library of Pittsburgh as a case example, this paper discusses three key ideas:

1. Patron needs arising within the technology transfer process;
2. Information resources that facilitate that process; and
3. Services provided to bring patrons into contact with the information they need.

The discussion focuses on the types of materials and services most useful to The Carnegie Library of Pittsburgh and its users in facilitating technology transfer.

TECHNOLOGY TRANSFER AND PUBLIC LIBRARIES

Technology transfer is the systematic translation of a technology from its point of development in one geographic area or industry to

Cheryl Engel is Reference Librarian in the Science and Technology Department, The Carnegie Library of Pittsburgh, 4400 Forbes Avenue, Pittsburgh, PA 15213. She has a BA from Pennsylvania State University and MLS from the University of Pittsburgh. She is a native of Pittsburgh and former Peace Corps volunteer, refugee relief worker, and interviewer of displaced steel workers.

its point of application in a secondary area or industry. To be successful technology transfer must occur at many levels, from development engineer to manager to worker, who must both learn the technology and provide the feedback necessary for its improvement and refinement. Implicitly, this requires access to technical information.

Public libraries facilitate technology transfer by providing access to scientific and technical literature, in formats and styles useful to the library's various publics, ranging from reference encyclopedias, bibliographic sources and theoretical books to patents, standards and specifications, shop manuals, trade catalogs, and late-breaking industry news. Public libraries provide the dual services of building scientific and technical collections, and directing patrons to the information that is useful to them. The transfer of information is provided through strong regional collection development and good patron service.

THE CARNEGIE LIBRARY IN CONTEXT: INDUSTRIAL HERITAGE, TECHNOLOGICAL TRANSFORMATION, AND PATRON NEEDS

Industrial Heritage

For almost two centuries Pittsburgh has been a major center for American mining, transportation, and manufacturing. Situated at the head of the Ohio River, blessed with abundant natural resources and a temperate climate, Pittsburgh in its early decades was the center of ironmaking, glassmaking, textile production, and commerce. By the 1880's Pittsburgh was the nation's leading producer of iron and steel, and a center of coal mining, oil production, heavy manufacturing, and finance. In 1950 Pittsburgh was the twelfth most populous city in the United States, the headquarters of a number of the nation's largest corporations, including U.S. Steel, Gulf Oil, Westinghouse, Alcoa, PPG, H.J. Heinz, and Mellon Bank.

Pittsburgh's rich industrial heritage has provided a fertile ground of support and demand for science and technology library services. The Carnegie Library of Pittsburgh was founded in 1892 with a building endowment from steel magnate Andrew Carnegie and appropriations from the citizens of Pittsburgh. In 1905 the library became the first major public library in the nation to establish a separate Science and Technology Department. Pittsburgh's industrial wealth also founded or enriched Pittsburgh's two major universities, Carnegie-Mellon University and the University of Pittsburgh, and several smaller universities or colleges. Carnegie Library with the two university libraries, forms the nexus for a regional web of scientific and technical libraries that include several dozen special libraries and corporate research centers, and a number of outstanding hospitals.

Technological Transformation

Pittsburgh, like many northeastern industrial cities during the 1960's and 1970's, suffered from population and industrial decline. These trends reached a climax in 1981-84, when the steel industry collapsed. Pittsburgh's industrial economy faced difficulties unseen since the Great Depression. Unemployment reached 15% in Pittsburgh and 25% in many milltown communities. Over 70,000 steelworkers and 95,000 other manufacturing workers—one-sixth of the entire regional labor force—lost their jobs. Overall, within the past ten years almost one-fourth of the currently non-retired residents of Allegheny County (22%) lost a job due to a plant closing, a mass layoff, a reorganization or downsizing, or became eligible for unemployment compensation with no expectation of returning to their previous occupation.

Management as well as workers suffered. Most major corporations reduced their management staffs, and those which did not lived in fear of the wave of mergers and acquisitions that swept the 1980's. In 1984, Chevron bought Gulf Oil, Pittsburgh's largest corporation, and moved the headquarters staff to San Francisco on a few months notice. Researchers who decided not to leave scrambled to find positions with other area companies, establish their own businesses or become consultants. State extended unemployment benefits also expired in 1984 for most former steel workers. Most had to learn a new livelihood. Managers and workers alike found in the library useful introductions to new technologies.

Even as the old order was collapsing, a new one was emerging. High technology, finance, education, health care, trade and services activities expanded and manufacturing contracted. Non-manufacturing jobs have increased in the 1980's, from 668,400 jobs in 1975 to 769,800 jobs in 1987. Pittsburgh's economy, once strongly specialized in manufacturing, is now similar to the national average in occupational and sectoral distribution. Pittsburgh's universities and hospitals have expanded dramatically during the 1980's. Carnegie Mellon University has consolidated its pre-eminent position as a computer sciences research center. This rapid growth has fostered many start-up ventures in computer, pharmaceutical, and biomedical industries.

In 1982, the Pittsburgh High Technology Council was formed to support start-up ventures in high technology. As of 1989, more than 700 firms and 70,000 employees were involved in Pittsburgh's advanced technology industry. Areas of concentration include industrial automation, advanced materials, software engineering and biomedical technology.

Patron Needs

Throughout its history Pittsburgh has been a major center of technological innovation and transfer. The success of technology transfer has depended, not on individuals, but on interdependent relations between several types of individuals:

1. Researchers and inventors, who conceptualize innovations;
2. Applications engineers, who actualize technologies;
3. Business managers and other supporting professionals, who provide the venture capital to make new ideas work;
4. Production workers, who provide the skilled labor necessary for industrial progress; and
5. Students, our key to future competitiveness.

CARNEGIE LIBRARY AS A FACILITATOR OF TECHNOLOGY TRANSFER

The Science and Technology Department serves local and regional patrons directly and through local libraries and is the state-designated resource center in science and technology. The Science and Technology Department occupies the third floor of the main library building in the Oakland section of Pittsburgh. The other departments at our Oakland location include Social Sciences, Humanities, Music and Art, Pennsylvania and Children's. Our Business Department is located in the Downtown section of Pittsburgh. The Library is situated directly between and within one block of the Carnegie-Mellon University and the University of Pittsburgh campuses.

The core science and technology collection includes:

> 380,000 books (circulating and reference)
> 425,000 bound periodical volumes
> 870,000 reels of microfilm and microfiche
> 150,000 technical reports
> 100,000 government documents
> 25,000 technical translations
> 22,000 trade catalogs
> 75,000 topographic maps
> 2,000 subscription journals and serials.

As a public library and a research collection, the Science and Technology Department is committed to supplying technical information at all levels. We assist scientists and inventors with literature and patent searches. We serve corporations applying innovative technologies in the marketplace by providing them with technical information. We provide government contractors with specifications necessary to get Federal and military contracts.

As one of 65 Patent and Trademark Depository Libraries in the United States, we provide access to almost five million United States patents. We also have a complete collection of British Patents. Our standards collection includes standards issued by the American National Standards Institute, all Federal standards and non-"controlled distribution" military specifications, all British standards, current and historical ASTM standards, the English translations of the German Institute for Standardization (DIN) standards and many other sets of standards published by government agencies (i.e., FCC, FAA, OSHA) and standards issuing bodies (i.e., SAE, AWS, API).

Our journal collection is extensive. We house more than 425,000 bound volumes on-site with additional holdings at our warehouse. Our journal selection ranges from highly technical journals to popular science publications. Endowments and contributions from the Pittsburgh Chapters of the American Chemical Society, the Spectroscopy Society, and the Society of Analytical Chemists and local science and technology corporations have supported many of our technical journal holdings. We subscribe to a wealth of industry specific journals as well as science and technology news magazines for our student users.

As the state-designated resource center in science and technology and a government depository library, we select a wide variety of reference materials supporting technology transfer at all levels. These include conference proceedings, handbooks, directories, subject-specific dictionaries and encyclopedias and technical reports. As a Department of Energy depository, we receive all DOE contract research documents on microfiche. We also hold an extensive collection of more than NASA technical reports. These two collections alone total more than 800,000 microfiche.

Services

The Library is open to the public from 9AM until 9PM all weekdays except Thursday, from 9AM until 5:30PM on Thursdays and Saturdays. Reference service is provided to walk-in patrons and telephone callers during these hours. The Library is also open on Sundays from 1PM until 5PM from mid-September until mid-May for walk-in service only. The Science and Technology reference desk is staffed by professional librarians during every hour the library is open, enabling evening and weekend access to technical and patent information.

As the regional resource center in science and technology, the department provides technical information to corporate and industrial researchers, university students and faculty, technical school students, school students and the public at large. Each of these user types has its own needs and receives services customized to these needs.

Corporate and industrial researchers are the heaviest users of our patents, standards and specifications, technical reports and our on-line searching and photocopy services. These users include researchers and engineers employed by large and medium-sized corporations, consultant-engineers, attorneys and chemists. Those who perform their research in the library work fairly independently once they become familiar with the Department's resources. They use our reference staff for assistance with identification of sources, selection of appropriate indexes and on-line databases in fields apart from their primary area of expertise. Many are regular users.

Our prime location between the University of Pittsburgh and Carnegie-Mellon University has resulted in heavy use of our collection by science and engineering students from both academic settings. Our journals, conference proceedings and technical reports receive heavy use by university students. Both universities have incorporated patents into their design engineering curricula. Students are required to perform a patent search in their area of interest as part of the course requirement. They perform these searches using the printed indexes and CASSIS CD-ROM in our patent searching area. Once these students become aware of the wealth of information available through the patent literature, patents become a standard part of their research for subsequent courses. Some of these engineering students have applied for and received patents in their area of interest prior to graduating. University students also have access to our on-line public access catalog from their respective university libraries.

The use of our collection by technical school students has increased dramatically in the 1980's. Traditionally the technical schools recruited their students from high schools. In the 1980s, a substantial number of technical school students were displaced workers. They are skilled workers in transition from one area of technical expertise to a new area of technical expertise. This trend seems to be continuing into the 1990's. Many of the technical schools in the Pittsburgh area require library research. Students arrive at the Department in groups for tours and stay for research. They often return in evenings and on weekends to finish their research projects. For many of these users, this is their first attempt at library research. We try to make it a successful one by guiding them to useful indexes and books. Some of the most popular subjects of research in our department include mechanics, electronics, heating refrigeration and air conditioning, robotics, aviation, and health-related topics.

The increase in emphasis on science and mathematics in education is reflected in increased usage of our department by middle and high school students. Science and invention fairs and contests have been highly popular in the Pittsburgh region. City and suburban schools send students to the library for research field trips. Last year, we gave tours to 1,222 students from urban and suburban schools. Because the research time is limited by bus schedules, many of these students do not finish their research and return during evenings and on weekends with their parents. All school systems have access to our library's book holdings on CD-ROM through the ACCESS PENNSYLVANIA program.

BUILDING BRIDGES—NOT BARRIERS— TO INFORMATION ACCESS

The Carnegie has joined forces with local and regional libraries to bridge access to information at both the local and state levels. In 1987, the Oakland Library Consortium was formed between The Carnegie Library of Pittsburgh, The University of Pittsburgh Libraries, and Carnegie-Mellon University Libraries to promote resource sharing and to enable access to the materials and services of the member libraries.

In 1985, the ACCESS Pennsylvania program was initiated. This program enables any Pennsylvania resident who is in good standing with his/her local library to borrow circulating materials from any state-supported library. Borrowers have the option of returning the materials to the loaning libraries or to their local library. This service subsidizes loaning libraries for materials borrowed. Increasingly, patrons from neighboring counties come to the library and take advantage of accessing technical materials directly and borrowing them at no cost.

In 1986, the first ACCESS PA CD-ROM was issued with current

holdings of The Carnegie Library of Pittsburgh and the holdings of school district libraries across the state. The newest disk contains the bibliographic holdings of 340 school, public, academic, special and government libraries. School students and faculty can use this service to identify materials to support research projects. These materials may then be borrowed using interlibrary loans or used at the owning library.

USAGE STATISTICS – MEASURING SUCCESS

Usage of the Science and Technology Department for both walk-in service and telephone reference has remained stable over the last ten years despite local and regional population declines. Our department continues to answer an average of 66,000 science and technology reference queries annually. In 1984, our usage increased by 20 percent. It is no coincidence that 1984 was the year that Gulf Oil was taken over by Chevron and most millworkers' extended unemployment benefits expired. For those who had continued to hope to return to the mills, retraining became a reality. This economic transition resulted in the need for information which in turn resulted in increased use of our library.

In the second half of 1989, the Patent and Trademark Depository Library Program began cumulating usage statistics from its CASSIS CD-ROM terminals. These statistics were extracted from the computers directly and assembled by total file accesses and total time using the patent search system. The Carnegie Library of Pittsburgh led the country in total number of patent searches with 1,851 searches from July through December 1989 (the first statistical period recorded), and we ranked second only to the McKinney Engineering Library at the University of Texas at Austin in total search time (800+ hours). Our patent collection and searching facilities receive heavy usage during both business and evening/weekend hours.

Our on-line searching statistics have increased steadily over the last ten years. Science and industry related on-line searches are provided by the Science and Technology librarians. Our librarians search DIALOG, STN, and ORBIT on a cost recovery basis. Researchers are charged the system-estimated cost of the search. In

1989, we performed 446 searches for businesses. Eighty-five percent of our on-line search time was spent performing customized searches for researchers. The remaining time was spent augmenting our reference services.

FUTURE PERSPECTIVES – PUBLIC LIBRARIES AS TRANSFER CENTERS

What does the future hold for public libraries and the transfer of technologies? In today's global marketplace technological transitions will increase with economic competition. The educational climate and access to information will be determining factors for developing, relocating, and expanding companies. Public libraries have traditionally provided unrestricted access to information. Regional efforts must continue for the dissemination of science and technology information. Large public libraries must work with university libraries to assure that technical information is available at all levels needed to promote regional economic development.

The transfer of technical information results in the transfer of technology and technology transfer results in jobs . . . new and different jobs! Job security was redefined for Pittsburghers in the 1980's. The Pittsburgh region continues to be a region in technological transition at the workplace level. In neighboring Westmoreland County, the Volkswagen automotive plant which closed in July 1988 resulting in 2,500 job losses will reopen in 1992 as a Sony television tube plant employing 2,000 skilled workers. In 1985, a Job and Career Education Center was created as part of the library's Humanities Department, incorporating the already exsisting Job Information Center and Education Information Center. In 1989, this Center served more than 19,000 patrons.

Technology transfer is not a single event nor a simple process of stimulus and response. It is a complex process growing from numerous individual acts of learning and creativity. These acts occur at all points of the transfer process, from initial testing to full-scale productivity, and at all work levels from researcher to production worker. Carnegie Library has sought to facilitate technology transfer by providing technical information at all levels.

REFERENCES

Allegheny County Work Force Issues and Unemployment Survey. Princeton NJ: The Gallup Organization, 1989. 142 pp.

Pittsburgh Facts 1988/1989: A Statistical Guide to the Pittsburgh Metropolitan Region. Greater Pittsburgh Office of Promotion, 1989.

Lorant, Stefan et al. *Pittsburgh: The Story of an American City*. Lenox, MA: Author's Edition, 1988. 736 pp.

SPECIAL PAPER

Supernova 1987A:
A Case Study of the Flow of Information
in the Literature of Astronomy
and Physics

Virgil Diodato

SUMMARY. An analysis of 877 documents from the primary literature and 2,408 references from the secondary literature of Supernova 1987A demonstrates the variety of material published on a scientific topic. For each type of periodical and each type of document there is an identifiable period when it is a major source of information about the topic.

INTRODUCTION

The Supernova

One hundred sixty thousand years ago, a star exploded in the Large Magellanic Cloud, a galaxy of stars near our own Milky Way

Virgil Diodato is Assistant Professor, University of Wisconsin-Milwaukee, School of Library and Information Science, P.O. Box 413, Milwaukee, WI 53201. He holds a PhD in Library and Information Science from the University of Illinois at Urbana-Champaign.

Acknowledgement is due to Tony Stankus, Editor of the SCI-TECH COLLECTIONS Section, for his work in identifying and critiquing this Special Paper.

101

Galaxy. The light from that explosion, or supernova, reached Earth on February 23, 1987. Because of the size and relative nearness of the explosion, astronomers now have had an opportunity to study the brightest supernova seen from this planet in hundreds of years.

The explosion is known variously as Supernova Shelton (for the first astronomer to report its discovery), the Supernova in the Large Magellanic Cloud, and SN1987A (for the first supernova discovered in 1987).

This astronomical event has been so important and so visible that already a large literature dealing with it has accumulated. The explosion of this star is reflected in an explosion of publications. As unique as the event itself is the opportunity to trace this group of publications from their very beginnings.

Purpose of the Paper

The purpose of this paper is to demonstrate the variety of publications that can deal with a scientific topic, in this case a supernova. The paper's purpose also is to demonstrate how there is a specific time for each type of publication to be a major source of information, whether it be a newspaper story or a scholarly research article or some other item.

Why use this event as the subject of such a case study? A case study is appropriate because of the importance of the event. SN1987A provides the best chance ever had by astronomers to test their theories about supernovae. And the explosion has even created a new subject field for astronomers and physicists. This new field is the study of neutrino particles emitted from a source outside our galaxy. This all means a great deal of communication in the literature of astronomy and physics, as well as in other communication channels such as meetings.

The importance to us of SN1987A is seen in the fact that there is already a small collection of publications about the literature of SN1987A. The first such contribution in library and information science was Stern's bibliography on SN1987A and other supernovae.[1] Other bibliographies aimed at amateur astronomers have appeared, including that by Fraknoi.[2] There have been essays on how the popular press has reported this event. See Schorn's commentary, for example.[3]

METHODOLOGY

Basics of the Method

The basic method has been to examine personally as many publications as possible about SN1987A. The examination period covered about two years. I looked at items published from the date of discovery, February 24, 1987, through February 28, 1989. Because this was such a short period, I focused my efforts on finding primary literature, which consisted of such items as periodical articles. To a lesser extent, the study examined some secondary literature (references in indexing and abstracting tools), and tertiary literature (dissertations and other monographs).

It certainly was not feasible to personally examine all or perhaps even most of the material on SN1987A that was published during this period. However, even my incomplete search demonstrates the variety of material that has been published. Importantly, every periodical included in this study has been examined thoroughly. I have searched each of these periodicals during its entire run from February 24, 1987 through February 28, 1989. For example, although only six daily newspapers are reported on here, how much and when they covered SN1987A ought to be typical of many newspapers in the United States.

Some Definitions

The "examined" primary literature discussed below are those publications that I personally examined. The primary publications were found in various periodicals. No mention is made in this analysis of the periodicals that I examined but in which I found nothing about SN1987A. Also not mentioned are periodicals for which I was able to examine only part of the run from February, 1987 through February, 1989.

The "major" publishing period for a periodical was the period of consecutive months during which it produced at least half of its total examined articles or other documents.

The "moderate" publishing period for a periodical was any month (other than a "major" month) during which the periodical produced at least three percent of its total examined articles or other documents.

The "minor" publishing period for a periodical was any month other than its "major" and "moderate" months.

Similar major, moderate, and minor distinctions are made in this paper for types of documents (such as research letters) and secondary sources (such as periodical indexes).

RESULTS AND DISCUSSION — PRIMARY LITERATURE

When Did Most of the Primary Literature About SN1987A Occur?

Most of the publications about SN1987A that were examined in this study appeared during the first ten months after discovery of the supernova. Publication slowed during the next fourteen months. For the entire twenty-four month period I examined 877 articles, newsnotes, observers' reports, and other primary documents. Slightly more than half the publications — 448 items — appeared between February 24 and the end of December, 1987. The other 429 documents were spread over the fourteen months covering January, 1988 through February, 1989.

Such a pattern is most interesting when looked at in detail. There are actually four publication phases. One can see the phases by looking at publication rates, that is, the number of SN1987A publications that appeared per month. The phases included: (1) a very rapid, explosion of publications that appeared immediately after the discovery, followed by (2) a brief period of only moderate publication rates, then (3) a sustained period of large though not explosive rates, and finally, (4) a long era of slow, steady growth in the literature. Table 1 shows the publishing rates by listing the monthly publication totals as well as the cumulative percents of examined documents.

Phase I: (February through May, 1987) An explosion of primary literature publications. Initial publication was immediate and rapid. The earliest examined document appeared within hours of the supernova's discovery on February 24, 1987. Over the next four days, February 25-28, seventeen more documents appeared. On March 23, less than a month after the discovery, already ten percent of the two years collection of examined documents on SN1987A had been published. And by the end of May, 1987, the stack of publications reached 185 items or twenty-one percent of the eventual total. Another way to look at the explosion is to realize that the March, 1987 publication rate of seventy-eight items averages more than two publications per day. And even though April, 1987 was the month with the slowest publication rate during this phase, there were still forty publications in the thirty days of that month.

Among the 185 items appearing in Phase I were documents from all the types of primary literature to be seen during the study. There were observers' circulars, newspapers, news magazines, general science periodicals, and journals from specific fields of science, namely astronomy and physics.

Phase II: (June through August, 1987) Moderate publication rates. For the three months of Phase II there were thirty-four to thirty-five publications per month. By the end of this phase, August 31, 1987, the accumulation of publications reached 289 items.

Phase III: (September, 1987 through February, 1988) Sustained period of large, though not explosive publishing rates. These six months produced steady literature growth. So, in Phase III five of the six months produced at least forty publications each. By the end of February, 1988, sixty percent or 531 of the examined documents had appeared in print.

Phase IV: (March, 1988 through February, 1989) Slow, steady publication rates. Starting immediately with March, 1988, and continuing for twelve months through the end of the study period, February 28, 1989, the publishing rates slowed. During Phase IV, almost every month had no less than eighteen but no more than

TABLE 1. The Primary Literature of SN1987A: Monthly Totals of Publications Appearing in Periodicals

Month	Number of Publications	Cumulative Percentage	Month	Number of Publications	Cumulative Percentage
2/87*	18	2	2/88	40	60
3/87	78	11	3/88	35	65
4/87	40	16	4/88	35	69
5/87	49	21	5/88	27	72
6/87	35	25	6/88	28	75
7/87	34	29	7/88	25	78
8/87	35	33	8/88	22	80
9/87	46	38	9/88	18	82
10/87	40	43	10/88	57	89
11/87	42	48	11/88	21	91
12/87	31	51	12/88	24	94
1/88	43	56	1/89	20	96
			2/89	34	100

*February 24-28, 1987.

thirty-five publications. With the end of Phase IV, the publications totaled 877 items.

How Did Various Publication Groups Contribute to These Publishing Patterns?

The publishing patterns mentioned above were caused by the amount of time it took each type of primary publication to respond to an event like the discovery of SN1987A. For example, newspapers can publish stories about an event a few hours or days after it occurs. There was an explosion of publications immediately following the discovery of SN1987A at least in part because newspapers, and some other primary publications, responded so quickly to the discovery.

Groups of Primary Publications

In this case study, I grouped the various primary publications into five types: astronomical circulars, daily newspapers, news magazines, general science periodicals, and astronomy and physics periodicals. There also was a small group of miscellaneous publications. The groupings allow us to see that each type of publication had its own time for focusing on SN1987A.

Figure 1 illustrates this by showing the major periods of publication during the twenty-four months of the study, for each group of primary publications. The "major" period was the time during which the group published at least half of its total of documents dealing with SN1987A. In Figure 1, the major period appears as a filled in block on each bar graph. Each publication group also had a moderate and a minor publication period. The graphs of Figure 1 are based on the data in Table 2. In the Methodology section above, there are definitions of "major," "moderate," and "minor" publication periods.

How the Groups of Primary Publication Give Explanations for the Primary Literature Publishing Patterns

The grouping of publications in Figure 1 and Table 2 provides explanations for the four phases mentioned earlier.

FIGURE 1. The Primary Literature of SN1987A: Publishing Periods, by Types of Periodicals

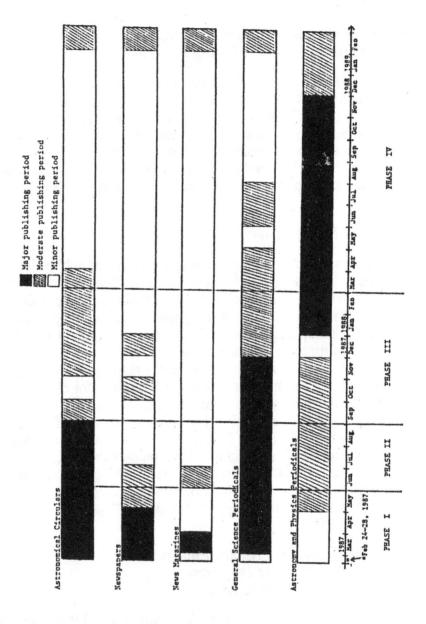

TABLE 2. The Primary Literature of SN1987A: Monthly Publication Totals, by Types of Periodicals

Month	Astron'l- Circulars	News Papers	News Magazines	General Science	Astronomy and Physics	Other
2/87*	9	8	0	1	0	0
3/87	29	18	5	15	11	0
4/87	15	6	0	9	10	0
5/87	11	3	0	8	27	0
6/87	6	4	1	8	16	0
7/87	8	1	0	10	15	0
8/87	5	0	0	7	23	0
9/87	8	1	0	14	23	3
10/87	4	2	0	13	21	0
11/87	8	1	0	13	20	0
12/87	6	4	0	7	14	0
1/88	7	1	0	10	25	0

TABLE 2 (continued)

2/88	6	1	0	7	26	0
3/88	7	1	0	7	20	0
4/88	4	0	0	6	24	1
5/88	6	0	0	4	17	0
6/88	2	1	0	7	18	0
7/88	2	0	0	7	16	0
8/88	1	1	0	4	16	0
9/88	1	0	0	2	12	0
10/88	2	0	0	3	52	0
11/88	4	0	0	0	17	0
12/88	4	0	0	0	20	0
1/89	2	0	0	3	15	0
2/89	6	3	1	7	17	0
Total:	163	56	7	172	475	4

*February 24-28, 1987.

Phase I. Figure 1 shows us that the major publication period for all the publication groups, except the astronomy and physics periodicals, occurred during the months of Phase I. This convergence of major publishing periods took place during the phase that covered the shortest period of time of all four phases. Also, March, 1987 was the peak month for four of the publication groups. The result was an explosion of publications.

Phase II. The slowing to moderate monthly publishing rates in Phase II occurred because this was the moderate or minor period for newspapers and news magazines. Even though astronomical circulars and general science periodicals were still in their major period during Phase II, they could no longer match their peak month of March, 1987.

Phase III. The return to large (though not explosive) monthly publication rates reflected the beginning of the major publication period for astronomy and physics periodicals. During this period all of the other groups, except for news magazines, also were in at least their moderate periods.

Phase IV. This slow and steady phase was dominated by the major publication period for astronomy and physics periodicals. That single group was able to maintain, with little exception, a publication level of fifteen to twenty-seven items per month. Nevertheless, the overall publication rate for all the groups was low because all the other groups of publications published little if anything during the months of Phase IV.

How Each Group of Primary Publications Demonstrated Its Own Importance to the Literature of SN1987A

Each publication played a role in disseminating information about SN1987A, almost regardless of when its major publication period occurred.

Astronomical Circulars (163 Items Published in 24 Months)

These publications are important because they rapidly report amateur and professional astronomers' observations about objects like new supernovae, comets, and variable stars. Some of the information is technical data about astronomical objects, and some of the information supports claims about who were the first discoverers of objects. My group of observers' circulars contains a single publication, the *International Astronomical Union (IAU) Circular*. I have placed the *AAVSO (American Association of Variable Star Observers) Circular* in another category. The *AAVSO Circular* series is called a "Circular" and does publish observers' reports, but it is published on a regular monthly, schedule, unlike the publish-as-needed schedule of the *IAU Circular*.

The earliest document about SN1987A appeared in issue number 4316 of the *IAU Circular* series. It was a typical though historic issue. This 3.5 inches by 5.5 inches card listed Ian Shelton as the first person to identify SN1987A. It provided his and others' observation data, such as brightness of the supernova and location in the sky. Issue 4316 reported "the discovery by Ian Shelton, University of Toronto Las Campanas Station [Chile], of a mag[nitude] 5 object, ostensibly a supernova in the Large Magellanic Cloud . . . . The discovery was made [on] February 24 . . . ."[4] Since this issue of the *IAU Circular* was dated February 24, this was an example of quite rapid publication.

As Figure 1 and Table 2 demonstrate, there were 163 reports devoted to SN1987A from the various circulars over the twenty-four months of the study. And more than half of those reports, eighty-three, appeared in February through August, 1987. Nine reports were published in the days right after discovery, February 24-28, and twenty-nine others in March, 1987. That is an important reason Phase I literature growth was so explosive.

Yet the circulars were of continuing importance to the literature, at least as measured by their frequency. One or more *IAU Circular* reports on SN1987A appeared during each of the twenty-four months of this study. And even as late as March 1988, the circulars were still in their moderate publishing period. The moderate activity, even months after discovery, is explained by the ongoing flow of new information about SN1987A. For example, in November 1987 through March 1988, astronomers were reporting findings on the gamma rays, neutrinos, and gravity waves emitted by the supernova.

Daily Newspaper (56 Items Published in 24 Months)

The daily newspaper is important because it provides information about an event soon after it happens and also because its stories are written to be understood by nonspecialists. I examined six daily, United States newspapers, which published fifty-six items about SN1987A.

Three articles in three different newspapers appeared on February 25, the day after discovery of SN1987A. Five other articles were published in February and eighteen more in March.

Over the study period, *The New York Times* published more articles than any of the other five dailies. Among its twenty-one articles was a page one story on the day after discovery, February 25, 1987. In its second sentence, this story foresaw that "this event is likely to have a dramatic effect on scientific understanding" of supernovae.[5]

The newspapers did most of their reporting almost immediately following the discovery of SN1987A. So, after June, 1987, there were only seventeen articles published in twenty months by the six papers. Even these were concentrated in several moderate publishing periods. For example, four articles were bunched together during December 17-21, 1987. At that time, an announcement about discoveries of emissions from SN1987A briefly reawakened newspaper interest in the supernova.[6]

News Magazines (7 Items Published in 24 Months)

The weekly news magazine provides coverage of major events within days of their occurrence. As is true for the newspaper, the news magazine tries to tell its stories in nontechnical terms. I looked at two of these weeklies that together published seven items about SN1987A.

Although there were only seven news magazine items on SN1987A during the two-year study period, five of them appeared in March, 1987. The most visible item and perhaps the one with the most information was *Time*'s cover story and editorial on March 23, 1987. The story contained lengthy descriptions, photographs, and diagrams of the supernova, a biography of an astronomer, and poetry from Robert Frost.[7]

General Science Periodicals (172 Items Published in 24 Months)

These are important publications for readers with good, general knowledge about various areas of science, whether or not the readers also are experts in specific fields of science. I examined eleven periodicals in this category.

This group stood out for the length of its major and moderate publishing periods. These sixteen months occurred during the long period from March, 1987 through July, 1988. Thus, general science periodicals contributed to moderate and large overall publishing patterns in Phases I, II, and III.

They also contributed to the slowing down of literature growth in Phase IV. Few if any items about SN1987A appeared in these periodicals in each month from August, 1988 through January, 1989.

Three of the most informative general science periodicals in this study were *Nature*, *The New Scientist*, and *Science News*. They respectively contributed eighty-six, thirty, and twenty-eight items, which totals more than half the 172 documents provided by the entire group of general science periodicals.

These three weeklies were especially interesting because they were both like and unlike the general science group as a whole. As was true for the entire group, the three publications produced rapid information about SN1987A in February and March of 1987. *Science News* was an especially rapid source. Its February 28, 1987 issue briefly mentioned SN1987A.[8] Daily newspapers and daily observers' circulars were the only other examined publications to produce documents about SN1987A in the same month as its discovery. *The New Scientist* and *Nature* also responded quickly, for they both had March 5, 1987 stories about the discovery.[9,10]

Science News, *The New Scientist*, and *Nature* were atypical general science periodicals because they continued to cover SN1987A throughout most of the months of the twenty-four month study period. This was unusual, for the general science periodicals, as a group, were in their minor publishing period after July, 1988. *Na-*

ture provided the best example of unusual continuity of coverage. There was at least one item per month in *Nature* on SN1987A for twenty-three of the twenty-four months of the study.

Evidence of the continuing coverage by the three weeklies was the fact that *The New Scientist* produced feature article cover stories on 1987A as late as November 5, 1987 and again on January 14, 1988, in addition to its sometimes weekly coverage of brief news about the supernova.[11,12]

Nature was impressive for the variety of its coverage. Consider September, 1987. Its weekly issues that month contained a newsnote about possible x-ray emissions from SN1987A,[13] a brief technical letter on detecting neutrinos from the supernova,[14] an essay that informally reviewed the first few months of discoveries,[15] and three scholarly reports of early research into SN1987A.[16]

Astronomy and Physics Periodicals
(475 Items Published in 24 Months)

These publications are important to those with a special interest in astronomy, whether they be amateur astronomers, professional researchers, or informed laypersons. I examined fifty of these periodicals. Their 475 documents on SN1987A were more than half of all the documents on SN1987A examined in all groups of primary publications during this study.

These periodicals affected the primary publication rates throughout the study period. They produced at least ten items per month, every month, from March, 1987 through February, 1989. Yet, their impact was most noticeable during Phase IV. The major publishing period (January through November, 1988) for these periodicals coincided almost exactly with the Phase IV era (March, 1988 through February, 1989). The steady production of primary literature on SN1987A during this time was due almost exclusively to the materials appearing in astronomy and physics periodicals.

There were both popular magazines and scholarly journals in the astronomy and physics periodicals group. Both types emphasized steady publication during Phase IV rather than rapid publication during Phase I. The amateur astronomer's *Astronomy* and *Sky & Telescope* produced eighteen items during Phase IV and only six during Phase I. And even the earliest of these six was rather late, an April, 1987 newsnote about the first few days of discovery and observation.[17]

Similarly, many scholarly periodicals took some time to review and produce technical articles on an event like SN1987A. And so, the most prolific scholarly source, *Astrophysical Journal*, did its publishing almost exclusively in Phase IV. Forty-three of its fifty-five items appeared during Phase IV, while not one item appeared during Phase I. Even its research letters section did not produce an item on SN1987A until a June 15, 1987 report on various spectra expected to be observed as more is learned about the supernova.[18]

However, not all of the specialized astronomy and physics periodicals published exclusively during Phase IV. A few of the periodicals were vital sources of information during Phase I. These included the *ESO (European Southern Observatory) Messenger*, *Astronomy and Astrophysics*, and *Physical Review Letters*. Together these three published twenty-five items about SN1987A during the February-May, 1987 days of Phase I. In fact, the *ESO Messenger* published its SN1987A items more frequently during Phase I than during any of the later phases. The nine items in its March, 1987 issue included observers' reports,[19] tabular data,[20] and a nontechnical article about the supernova.[21]

Astronomy and Astrophysics and *Physical Review Letters* were able to produce material during Phase I because of their use of research letters. This correspondence from astronomers and physicists demonstrated two characteristics of a scientific journal's research letters. They were reports of early research findings on SN1987A, and they were published relatively soon after being submitted to the journals. The first of the research letters from these two journals were about the determining of an accurate location for the supernova[22] and the initial detection of neutrinos from the supernova.[23]

Yet, as a group the fifty astronomy and physics periodicals that I examined indeed did focus their publishing activity during the final part of the study period, during Phase IV. Among these March, 1988-February, 1989 items were detailed research articles on some of the major aspects of SN1987A. These included research articles on which star was the one that exploded into SN1987A,[24] on the historical fact that SN1987A permitted "the first direct observation in neutrino astronomy,"[25] and on how SN1987A fit into current models of supernova categories.[26]

What Kinds of Documents Were Found in the Primary Literature?

The primary literature of a field often makes us think of journal articles. But there certainly are other types of documents that make up a primary literature. I subjectively categorized the 877 primary literature publications dealing with SN1987A into various document types. These document types were: research letters (221 documents examined), research articles (181), observers' reports (202), newsnotes (156), non-research articles (43), and miscellaneous documents (74). See Table 3.

There were patterns for when the various document types appeared. Figure 2, which is based on the data in Table 3, demonstrates which document types dominated during the four phases. Each document type had its "major" publishing period. This major period was the time when at least half of the documents of that type were published. In Figure 2, the major period appears as a filled in block on each bar graph. Each document type also had a moderate and a minor publication period; they, too, are indicated in Figure 2.

How the Document Types Provide Explanations for the Primary Literature Publishing Patterns

The information in Figure 2 and Table 3 provides explanations for the four phases mentioned earlier.

Phase I. Figure 2 shows us that observers' reports, newsnotes, and non-research articles all were in their major publishing period during Phase I. The large quantity of observers' reports and newsnotes, especially in March, 1987, provide a reason for the explosive nature of Phase I.

Phase II. Publication rates moderated during this period. A reason for the moderation is the fact that research articles, observers' reports, and newsnotes never again appeared in the abundance that they did in Phase I.

FIGURE 2. The Primary Literature of SN1987A: Publishing Periods, by Types of Documents

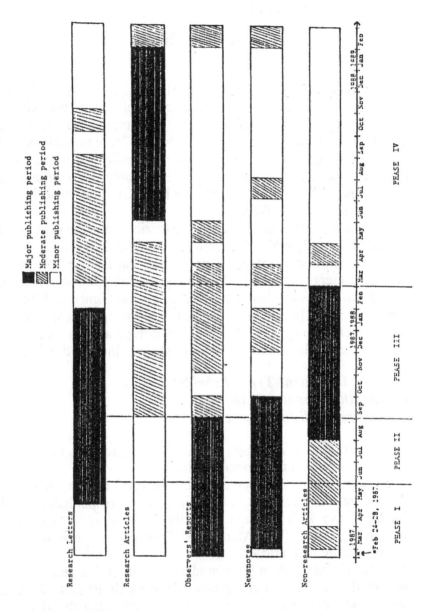

TABLE 3. The Primary Literature of SN1987A: Monthly Publication Totals, by Types of Documents

Month	Research Letters	Research Articles	Observers' Reports	News- Notes	NonResearch Articles	Other
2/87*	0	0	9	6	0	3
3/87	1	0	37	29	5	6
4/87	5	3	16	12	1	3
5/87	18	3	14	9	3	2
6/87	11	2	7	11	3	2
7/87	12	1	10	6	2	3
8/87	13	2	7	5	2	5
9/87	12	8	9	8	6	3
10/87	17	7	5	10	0	1
11/87	19	6	9	3	4	1
12/87	3	3	7	9	2	7
1/88	14	7	9	5	5	3

TABLE 3 (continued)

2/88	6	16	7	4	4	3
3/88	9	8	8	7	1	2
4/88	10	8	6	3	2	6
5/88	8	5	7	2	1	4
6/88	7	11	3	4	0	3
7/88	10	5	3	5	1	1
8/88	8	6	3	3	0	2
9/88	5	7	2	0	0	4
10/88	7	41	4	1	1	3
11/88	6	8	5	1	0	1
12/88	6	10	5	2	0	1
1/89	6	6	3	3	0	2
2/89	8	8	7	8	0	3
Total:	221	181	202	156	43	74

Phase III. Research letters dominated this period and help explain the large amount of publications during this time. The major publishing period for research letters ended at the same time that Phase III came to a close.

Phase IV. This slow publication period was reflected in the balancing of publishing periods for two document types. During Phase IV research articles left their moderate period and moved up to their major publishing period. But this increase was offset by the movement of the research letters group from its moderate down to a minor publishing period.

How Each Document Type Demonstrated Its Own Importance to the Literature of SN1987A

Each document type played a role in disseminating information about SN1987A, whatever its rate of publication during the twenty-four months of this study.

Research Letters (221 Items Published in 24 Months)

The research letter dominated all the other document types, both in number of items published and in the length of its major publishing period. It took a couple of months after the discovery of SN1987A for there to be a steady flow of research letters about the supernova. But once the flow began, research letters had a major publishing period that lasted a long time, from May, 1987 through January, 1988. And at least one research letter was published in every month of the study period, except for the month of discovery, February, 1987.

It is appropriate that a research letter appear shortly after the event that it discusses. A research letter looks very much like a research article appearing in a scientific journal, except that it is often relatively short. It is special also because it probably has taken less time to get published than the typical research article. Quick yet formal publication of early research results on some phenomenon or event is the purpose of the research letter.

This author identified these letters in two ways. First, any signed document in a journal labeled as a letters journal was considered a research letter. For material on SN1987A, *Physical Review Letters* and *Physics Letters* were important examples of such journals. Second, any document in a journal's "Letters" section was considered a research letter, as long as the section was not actually a collection of opinion or commentary items. *Nature*'s "Letters to Nature" as well as the "Letters" sections of *Astronomy and Astrophysics* and of the *Astrophysical Journal* were such sources for SN1987A.

The earliest research letter I examined appeared in early April. In one and a half pages it discussed the detection some five weeks earlier of neutrinos from SN1987A.[27] Considering that the study period covered only the first two years following the discovery of SN1987A, it is quite proper that research letters were the primary document type used to report this event.

Research Articles (181 Items Published in 24 Months)

It is not surprising that the major publishing period for this document type did not occur until Phase IV. We expect it to take at least a few months for researchers to do and report their research and for their manuscripts to be processed by scientific journals. As Figure 2 shows, research articles began their major publishing period in June, 1988, fifteen months after the supernova's discovery. No other document type had to wait so long to reach its major publishing period.

A research article was a document (other than a research letter) reporting research on SN1987A, aimed at an audience of other researchers, and almost always having references to articles from the astronomy and/or physics literature.

The typical research article on SN1987A appeared in an astronomy or physics journal. Examples include articles noted in the Astronomy and Physics Periodicals section above.[24,25,26]

The most abundant sources of research articles on SN1987A were: *Proceedings of the Astronomical Society of Australia*, *Physical Review D*, and *Astrophysical Journal*. Research articles were found outside such specialized journals, though this occurred very infrequently. General science sources like *Nature* and *Publications of the National Academy of Sciences* did publish some research articles on SN1987A.

What is most important about the pattern of research articles is what we have not seen yet. Surely, more than any of the other document types, the research articles on SN1987A will continue to appear for many years into the future.

Observers' Reports (202 Items Published in 24 Months)

As noted above, 163 of the observers' reports appeared in the *IAU Circular* series. Because these circulars provide rapid publication services, the major publishing period for observers' reports began immediately in the month of discovery, February, 1987.

Other sources of observers' reports included: *AAVSO Circular*, *Australian Journal of Astronomy*, *ESO Messenger*, and *Information Bulletin on Variable Stars*. Many of these other observers' reports included data similar to that found in an astronomical circular. However, publication of a report by a monthly astronomical journal is definitely not as rapid as daily publication by a circular.

Newsnotes (156 Items Published in 24 Months)

Because they delivered news about SN1987A, many of these newsnotes appeared soon after the discovery. The major publishing period for this document type extended from March through September of 1987, and, by far, the most prolific month was March, 1987. As SN1987A became less important as a news item, these documents appeared less frequently, with very few being published after July, 1988.

The author identified a newsnote by what it was not and what it was. It was not a piece of research. It was not a feature article in a periodical. A newsnote was news. It briefly described a recent, specific event about SN1987A. It usually appeared in the news section of a general science periodical or an astronomy periodical aimed at amateur astronomers.

Science News produced four newsnotes in February and March of 1987 that reported the early sightings of the supernova.[28] In September, 1987, *Astronomy* used a newsnote to summarize recent conference papers for its amateur astronomer readers.[29] And, in one of the last documents I viewed during the study, *Sky & Telescope* published a newsnote in February, 1989, to report the fading away of the brightness of SN1987A.[30]

Non-Research Articles (43 Items Published in 24 Months)

Often aimed at the nonspecialist individual who is interested in astronomy, these items provided something more than a newsnote and something less than a technical research article. The non-research article had its major publishing period during August, 1987 through February, 1988. That nicely spanned most of the time between the end of the major publishing period for newsnotes and the beginning of the major period for research articles. A reprise of the first two hundred days of SN1987A in *Sky & Telescope* was an example of the non-research article.[31] Other good sources of the non-research article on SN1987A included *Astronomy* and *Physics Today*.

Miscellaneous Other Documents (74 Items Published in 24 Months)

Included in the miscellany were opinion pieces, items that mentioned SN1987A only in passing, photographic essays, and errata.

This unusual supernova stimulated the writing of editorials, letters to the editor, essays, and other opinion pieces. I found thirty-four of these. There was the newspaper editorial that said "even [stars] are not forever."[32] There was the letter to a journal editor describing an astronomer who might have sighted SN1987A before its official discoverer did. The competitor's report was "delayed. By the time I did obtain confirmation, the cat was out of the bag."[33] And there was the essay on the "serendipitous way" that the discovery of SN1987A led to the founding of the discipline of "extra-galactic observational neutrino astronomy."[34]

Perhaps the most intriguing documents in the miscellany were those that happened to give only very brief mention to SN1987A, usually in a single sentence, and then never refer to it again. The twenty-six documents found with what I call "in-passing" comments attest to the pervasiveness and importance of SN1987A. They clearly assumed the reader knew about the event.

These in-passing comments occurred within various types of documents. For purposes of this study, I disregarded whether the document was, say, a research article or a non-research article. If the mention of SN1987A was very brief and only peripheral to the main topic of the publication, I categorized the item as being in-passing.

Some of these in-passing comments told how SN1987A indeed affected the flow of research itself. "The explosion of SN1987A has given added excitement and importance to the study of supernova physics . . . ."[35] "Studies of Supernova 1987A . . . have given us the confidence that our basic understanding of stars . . . may not be too far off."[36] "The proximity of the recent Type II Supernova 1987a . . . should give us an unprecedented opportunity to observe. . . ."[37] Each of the three preceding sentences was the only comment about SN1987A in their respective articles.

The very nature of in-passing material made them retrievable only by browsing or intensely looking through every item in an astronomy or physics periodical.

After opinion pieces and in-passing comments, the remnants of the miscellany included fourteen other items that were either errata in astronomy and physics journals or photographic essays in the amateur astronomy periodicals.

What Other Kinds of Documents Were in the Primary Literature?

There were at least three other types of documents in the primary literature about SN1987A. These are perhaps the most difficult to control bibliographically, and it was not feasible for the author to attempt to examine these items. They included: conference papers, technical reports, and preprints. A reader of the literature on SN1987A quickly becomes aware of these sources because of the frequency with which they appear in the bibliographies of journal articles.

Conference Papers. Examining the bibliographies of articles in scholarly journals made it clear that conferences were rapidly called to discuss this event. Some of the conference papers about SN1987A are indeed counted among the 877 items discussed above. This is because some conference papers also were printed as articles within issues of journals. For more information about conference papers on SN1987A, see the discussion below on indexes of special materials in the section on Secondary Literature.

Technical Reports. Technical reports on SN1987A were issued by universities, observatories, laboratories, and other places where astronomers and physicists do their work. Some of these also appeared as conference papers but probably not as journal articles. For more information about technical reports on SN1987A, see the discussion below on indexes of special materials in the section on Secondary Literature.

Preprints. A preprint is an early draft of a research paper sent by an author to colleagues who share that author's research interests. A preprint can be delivered informally through channels like surface mail and electronic mail. A preprint also can be delivered formally, as when it is part of a preprint series published by a university, laboratory, or other organization. Although this case study does not analyze preprints, it was not unusual to find references to such material in the journal literature.

RESULTS AND DISCUSSION – SECONDARY LITERATURE

When Did Most of the Secondary Literature About SN1987A Occur?

The very nature of periodical indexes and other secondary literature forces them to appear usually sometime after their primary literature. And so, the highest monthly publication totals for references found in the secondary literature occurred months after the explosion of the primary literature. I found 2,408 references to SN1987A in seven secondary sources. About half of the references appeared in the final eight months (July, 1988 through February, 1989) of the twenty-four month study period. This was one characteristic of the secondary literature publishing pattern.

A second characteristic of the secondary literature on SN1987A was the slow but steady growth of the monthly totals of references from zero in February, 1987 to 121 in August, 1987.

A third characteristic was the major influence of one tool, *Astronomy and Astrophysics Abstracts*, which by itself produced more than half of all the references found. The relative influence of this one tool was caused in part by there being only seven secondary sources examined. Yet, this indeed is a major secondary tool in this field, and it is appropriate for it to dominate.

Note that if an article on SN1987A was indexed by, for example, both *General Science Index* (GSI) and *Physics Abstracts* (PA), then that reference is included in both the tallies for GSI and for PA in this analysis.

How Did Each Secondary Publication Contribute to This Publishing Pattern?

The major publishing periods for the seven secondary sources are displayed in Figure 3. These graphs are based on the data in Table 4. See the Methodology section above for definitions of these publishing periods.

The seven secondary sources can be categorized as: indexes of the astronomy and physics literature, indexes of the general science literature, and indexes of special materials.

Indexes of the Astronomy and Physics Literature (1,877 References)

The overwhelming majority of the secondary references were in two sources: *Astronomy and Astrophysics Abstracts* (1,342 references) and *Physics Abstracts* (535 references). As a group, these two indexes produced most of their references on SN1987A during the period December, 1987 through September, 1988. Therefore, those ten months were the best time during which to find references to SN1987A.

The most prolific coverage of SN1987A by any source came in the February and August, 1988 issues of *Astronomy and Astrophysics Abstracts*. These 1,267 references provided a great deal of access to information about SN1987A.

Physics Abstracts' major publishing period occurred during De-

FIGURE 3. The Secondary Literature of SN1987A: Major Publishing Periods (filled-in blocks)

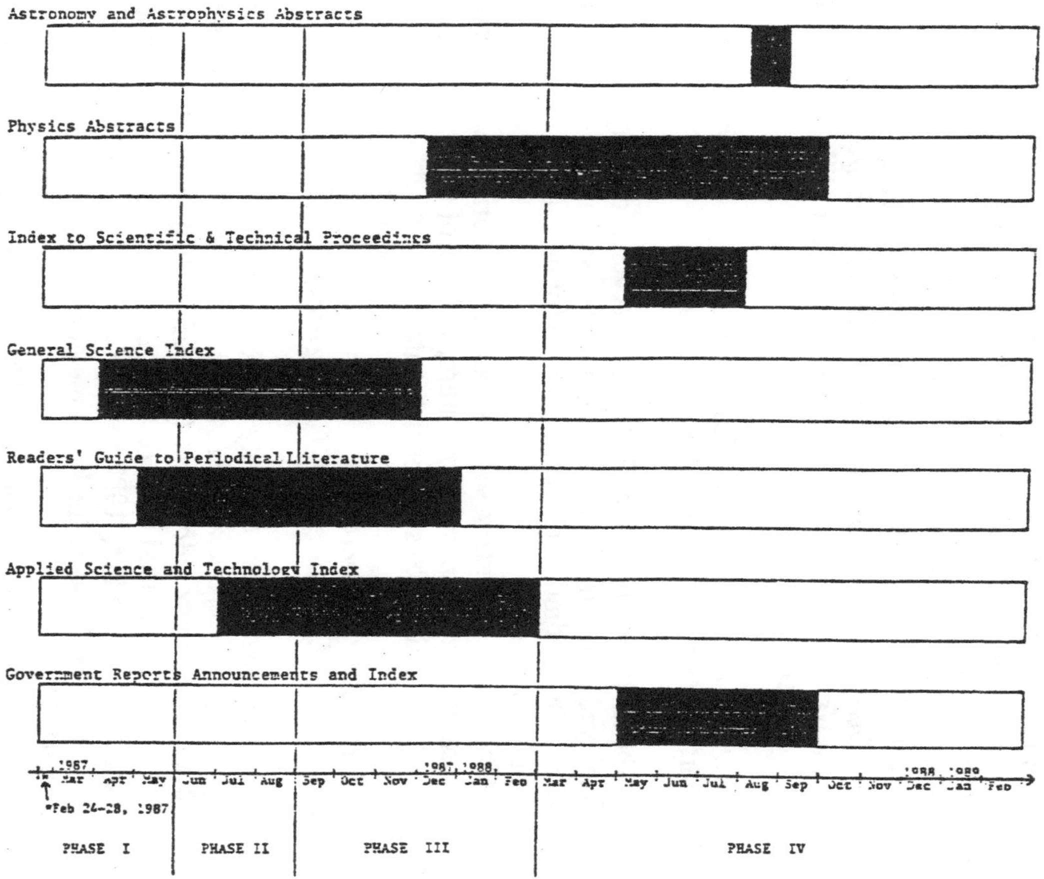

TABLE 4. The Secondary Literature of SN1987A: Monthly Entries in Indexing and Abstracting Sources

Month	AAA*	PA	ISTP	GS	RG	AST	GR	Monthly Total	Cumulative Percentage
3/87	--	0	0	0	6	5	0	11	0
4/87	--	0	0	17	2	3	0	22	1
5/87	--	0	0	9	5	2	0	16	2
6/87	--	12	0	4	8	3	0	27	3
7/87	--	29	0	12	8	5	0	54	5
8/87	75	28	0	14	4	0	0	121	10
9/87	--	27	0	7	6	2	0	42	12
10/87	--	25	0	15	3	3	0	46	14
11/87	--	18	0	13	4	4	0	39	16
12/87	--	24	0	17	6	5	1	53	18
1/88	--	25	0	4	9	2	1	41	20
2/88	370	25	3	11	3	6	1	419	37
3/88	--	31	0	9	3	2	0	45	39
4/88	--	33	75	10	4	3	0	125	44
5/88	--	29	2	2	4	1	3	41	46
6/88	--	40	4	6	2	0	4	56	48
7/88	--	24	93	5	2	2	0	126	53
8/88	897	24	1	5	4	1	1	933	92
9/88	--	34	0	5	0	1	2	42	94
10/88	--	20	3	3	1	0	0	27	95
11/88	--	18	0	2	1	0	1	22	96
12/88	--	23	0	0	0	0	1	24	97
1/89	--	25	15	1	2	1	0	44	99
2/89	--	21	2	2	1	1	5	32	100
Total:	1342	535	198	173	88	52	20	2408	

TABLE 4 (continued)

```
*AAA is published twice a year.

AAA is Astronomy and Astrophysics Abstracts; PA is Physics

Abstracts; ISTP is Index to Scientific & Technical Proceedings;

GSI is General Science Index; RG is Readers' Guide to Periodical

Literature; AST is Applied Science and Technology Index; GR is

Government Reports Announcements and Index.
```

cember, 1987 through September, 1988. And its grand total of 535 references were spread rather evenly, with little exception, among a much longer period, June, 1987 through February, 1989. This continuing, strong coverage of SN1987A makes *Physics Abstracts* a consistently important tool for this topic.

These two indexes were important also because they covered not only periodical articles, but also other sources, including monographs and conference papers. References to all types of publications are included in the data for these indexes in Table 4.

Indexes of the General Science Literature (313 References)

The other three periodical indexes examined were not as specialized in covering astronomy and physics as the two above. These more general sources were *General Science Index* (173 references), *Readers' Guide to Periodical Literature* (88), and *Applied Science and Technology Index* (52). Although they carried relatively few references, these three were important indexes for how rapidly they produced their references. Considering the three as a group, they produced most of their references during March through November, 1987. Thus, they served well for finding information about SN1987A prior to the prolific period for the two indexes of astronomy and physics literature.

Indexes of Special Materials (218 References)

The indexes in this group were *Index to Scientific & Technical Proceedings* (208 references) and *Government Reports Announce-*

ments and Index (20 references). As Table 4 and Figure 3 show, the most appropriate time to find material about SN1987A in these tools was during May through September of 1988.

Index to Scientific & Technical Proceedings was unusual among all the secondary and even some primary sources examined because of the wide difference from issue to issue in amounts of items covering SN1987A. Consider April through July of 1988. That four month period included one month with seventy-five references, two months with a total of only six references, and then a month with ninety-three references. Yet, that is the nature of conferences. Two of the months had many references because each covered conferences in which every paper in the conferences dealt with SN1987A.

Government Reports Announcements and Index referenced only twenty items on SN1987A. Informal examination of the bibliographies of primary literature articles on SN1987A suggests there were many more than twenty technical reports published. The few picked up by this index is evidence that technical reports are not as bibliographically controlled as many other types of publications.

What Other Secondary Publications Covered SN1987A?

There were other important secondary publications that contained references to SN1987A but were not examined for this study. As Stern mentions, two of the most appropriate are *Astronomy and Astrophysics Monthly Index* and *Science Citation Index*.[38]

There were still other, peripheral secondary sources that were not examined. A search of the CROS index to the BRS Search Service collection of online databases revealed some of these during a search in May, 1989. The search expression was "supernova$1 and 1987A." Among the fifteen databases that had at least one reference each were ERIC, the GPO Monthly Catalog, and PTS/PROMT. The search also verified that the INSPEC database, an online counterpart to *Physics Abstracts* (and to other printed indexes) is a major source of information about SN1987A. See Table 5. Please note that this May, 1989 online search probably contains references to primary material published after the February, 1989 deadline for this analysis.

TABLE 5. The Secondary Literature of SN1987A: An Online Search of the Expression "Supernova$1 and 1987A".

BRS Search Service Database	Number of Items Retrieved on May 18, 1989
AHCI: Arts & Humanities Search	1
BBIP: Books in Print	2
DALY: Newsearch	17
DISS: Dissertations Abstracts Online	4
ERIC: Educational Resources Information Center	2
GPOM: GPO Monthly Catalog	2
INSP: Inspec	708
MAGS: Magazine Index	58
MSAP: Magazines ASAP III	19
NOOZ: National Newspaper Index	7
NTIS: NTIS Bibliographic Database	43
OCLC: OCLC EASI Reference	9
PMRO: Popular Magazine Review Online	40
PTSL: PTS/PROMT-F&S Indexes	2
TSAP: Trade and Industry ASAP III	4

RESULTS AND DISCUSSION —
TERTIARY LITERATURE

Dissertations, annual reviews, and other monographs have been selected as tertiary publications. There was enough time for only a few of these to cover SN1987A before the February, 1989 deadline of this analysis. I examined seven of these tertiary publications.

Dissertations (2 items published). In 1988 at least two dissertations appeared that mentioned SN1987A in their abstracts. Both dealt with the spectra of supernovae.[39,40] It is possible that other dissertations published during the twenty-four month study period mentioned SN1987A in the text of the dissertations themselves.

Annual Reviews (3 items published). A scholarly review article on SN1987A appeared in the 1987 edition of the *Annual Review of Astronomy and Astrophysics*.[41] For the general science reader or amateur astronomer, one article appeared in each of the 1988 and 1989 editions of the *Yearbook of Astronomy*.[42,43]

Other Monographs (2 items published). Two books for the nonspecialist have been examined that dealt with SN1987A. Genet and others have SN1987A as their main topic,[44] while Marschall's book discusses SN1987A as one of many supernovae.[45]

NOTES

1. Stern, David. Supernovae: A Guide to the literature. *Science & Technology Libraries* 9(2):97-117; 1988 Winter.

2. Fraknoi, A. Supernovae. *Mercury*. 16(3):122-123; 1987 July/August.

3. Schorn, Ronald A. Supernova 1987A and the press. *Sky & Telescope*. 74(2):116; 1987 August.

4. Supernova 1987A in the Large Magellanic Cloud. *IAU Circular*. No. 4316; 1987 February 24.

5. Browne, Malcom W. Huge stellar explosion detected close enough for careful study. *The New York Times*. 136(47061):A1,A13(local edition); 1987 February 25.

6. Browne, Malcom W. Exploding stars shown to yield life elements. *The New York Times*. 136(47356):A29(local edition); 1987 December 17.

7. Lemonick, Michael D. Supernova! *Time*. 129:62-63, 65-67, 69; 1987 March 23.

8. Nearby supernova. *Science News* 31(9):132; 1987 February 28.

9. Henbest, Nigel. Exploding star startles astronomers. *The New Scientist*. 113(1550):14-15; 1987 March 5.

10. Campbell, P. Supernova almost on the doorstep. *Nature.* 326(6108):11; 1987 March 5.

11. Henbest, Nigel. Supernova: The Cosmic bonfire. *The New Scientist.* 116(1585):52-57; 1987 November 5.

12. Sutton, Christine. The Secret life of the neutrino. *The New Scientist.* 117(1595):53-57; 1988 January 14.

13. Supernova! *Nature.* 329(6134):3; 1987 September 3.

14. Barbiellini, Guido, and Giuseppe Cocconi. Electric charge of the neutrinos from SN1987A. *Nature.* 329(6134):21-22; 1987 September 3.

15. Murdin, Paul. Supernova 1987A: The Parent and its environs. *Nature.* 329(6134):12-13; 1987 September 3.

16. For example, see: Nussinov, S., and others. SN1987A supernova: A Black-hole precursor? *Nature.* 329(6135):134-135; 1987 September 10.

17. Schorn, Ronald A. A Supernova in our backyard. *Sky & Telescope.* 73(4):382; 1987 April.

18. McCray, Richard, and others. Inside Supernova 1987A. *Astrophysical Journal.* 317(2):L73-L77; 1987 June 15.

19. For example, see: Fosbury, R. The Spectrum of Supernova 1987A. *ESO Messenger.* No. 47:32-33; 1987 March.

20. Monderen, P., and others. Walraven photometry of Supernova 1987A. *ESO Messenger.* No. 47:27; 1987 March.

21. West, R. M. Chronology of a once-in-a-lifetime event. *ESO Messenger.* No. 47:30-31; 1987 March.

22. West, R. M., and others. Astronomy of SN 1987A and Sanduleak-69 202. *Astronomy and Astrophysics.* 177(1/2):L1-L3; 1987 May.

23. Hirata, K., and others. Observation of a neutrino blast from the supernova SN1987A. *Physical Review Letters.* 58(14):1490-1493; 1987 April 6.

24. Woosley, S. E. SN 1987A: After the peak. *Astrophysical Journal.* 330(1):218-253; 1988 July 1.

25. Hirata, K. S., and others. Observation in the Kamiokande-II detector of the neutrino burst from supernova SN1987A. *Physical Review D.* 38(2):448-458; 1987 July 15.

26. Van den Bergh, Sidney. A Possible correlation between the luminosities of supernovae of type II and the absolute magnitudes of their parent galaxies. *Astronomical Journal.* 96(2):701-703; 1988 August.

27. Bahcall, J. N., and S. L. Glashow. Upper limit on the mass of the electron neutrino. *Nature.* 326(6112):476-477; 1987 April 2.

28. For example, see: Thompsen, E. Neutrino astronomy born in a supernova. *Science News.* 131(12):180; 1987 March 21.

29. Nature of Supernova 1987A, mysterious companion discussed at AAS meeting. *Astronomy.* 15(9):74-75; 1987 September.

30. Supernova 1987A: Fading away. *Sky & Telescope.* 77(2):127 1989 February.

31. Schorn, Ronald A. Supernova 1987A after 200 days. *Sky & Telescope.* 74(5):477-479; 1987 November.

32. Last gasp is a real show. *Los Angeles Times*. II-4; 1987 February 26.

33. Henshaw, Colin. The Independent discovery of Supernova 1987A in the Large Magellanic Cloud, from Zimbabwe. *Quarterly Journal of the Royal Astronomical Society*. 28(4):533-534; 1987 December.

34. Bernstein, Jeremy. Out of my mind: SN 1987-A. *American Scholar*. 57(2):167-168,170-172; 1988 Spring.

35. Seidel, Edward, and others. Gravitational radiation from type-II supernovae. *Physical Review D*. 38(8):2349-2356; 1988 October 15.

36. Woltjer, Lodewijk. A World of opportunities in astronomy. *Sky & Telescope*. 76(4):116; 1988 October.

37. Chevalier, Roger A., and Craig L. Sarazin. Hot gas in the universe. *American Scientist*. 75(6):609-618; 1987 November/December.

38. Stern. Supernovae: A Guide to the literature. P. 116.

39. Jeffery, David John. *Supernova Polarization Spectra Calculated Using the Sobolev-H Method*. Hamilton, ON: McMaster University; 1988. Dissertation.

40. Pinto, Philip Alfred. *The Late-time Spectra of Supernovae*. Santa Cruz, CA: University of California, Santa Cruz; 1988. Dissertation.

41. Weiler, Kurt W., and Richard A. Sramek. Supernovae and supernova remnants. *Annual Review of Astronomy and Astrophysics*. 26:295-341; 1988.

42. Moore, Patrick. Supernova! *1988 Yearbook of Astronomy*. New York: Norton; 1987. Pp. 176-180.

43. Allen, David. A Bang in the night. *1989 Yearbook of Astronomy*. New York: Norton; 1988. Pp. 125-137.

44. Genet, Russell M., and others. *Supernova 1987A: Astronomy's Explosive Enigma*. Mesa, AZ: Fairborn; 1987.

45. Marschall, Laurence A. *The Supernova Story*. New York: Plenum; 1988.

APPENDIX

Primary Publications Examined,
Arranged by Group

Astronomical Circular

International Astronomical Union Circular

Daily Newspapers

Chicago Tribune
Christian Science Monitor
Los Angeles Times
The New York Times
The Wall Street Journal
The Washington Post

News Magazines

Time
U. S. News & World Report

General Science Periodicals

American Scientist
Natural History
Nature
The New Scientist
Popular Science
Publications of the National Academy of Sciences
Research and Development
Science
Science News
Smithsonian

Astronomy and Physics Periodicals

AAVSO Circular
Acta Astronomica Sinica
Aerospace America
Astronomical Journal
Astronomy
Astronomy and Astrophysics
Astrophysical Journal
Astrophysical Letters & Communications
Astrophysics and Space Science
Australian Journal of Astronomy
Aviation Week & Space Technology
Chinese Astronomy and Astrophysics

Astronomy and Physics Periodicals (continued)

Chinese Physics
Contemporary Physics
ESA Bulletin
ESO Messenger
Europhysics Letters
Helvetica Physica Acta
IEEE Transactions on Nuclear Science
Information Bulletin on Variable Stars
Irish Astronomical Journal
JETP Letters
Journal of Astrophysics and Astronomy
Journal of the Royal Astronomical Society of Canada
Mercury
Modern Physics Letters A
Monthly Notices of the Royal Astronomical Society
Nuclear Instrument & Methods in Physics Research A
Nuclear Physics A
Nuclear Physics B
Nuovo Cimento A
Nuovo Cimento B
Nuovo Cimento C
Physical Review D
Physical Review Letters
Physics Letters A
Physics Letters B
Physics Reports
Physics Today
Proceedings of the Astronomical Society of Australia
Progress of Theoretical Physics
Publications of the Astronomical Society of Japan
Publications of the Astronomical Society of the Pacific
Quarterly Journal of the Royal Astronomical Society
Reviews of Modern Physics
Soviet Journal of Nuclear Physics
Space Science Reviews
Space World
Zeitschrift fur Physik C

Other

American Scholar
National Geographic

NEW REFERENCE WORKS
IN SCIENCE AND TECHNOLOGY

Arleen N. Somerville, Editor

The reviewers for this issue are: Laura Delaney (LD), New York Public Library; Isabel Kaplan (IK), University of Rochester; Richard Kaplan (RK), Rensselaer Polytechnic Institute; Kathleen Kehoe (KMK), Columbia University; Donna Lee (DL), University of Vermont; Ellis Mount (EM), Columbia University; Diane J. Reiman (DJR), University of Rochester; Arleen N. Somerville (ANS), University of Rochester.

GENERAL SCIENCE

The Almanac of science and technology: what's new and what's known. Ed. by Richard Golob and Eric Bius. Boston: Harcourt Brace Jovanovich; 1990. 531p. $59.95 (pbk). ISBN 0-15-105050-3; 0-15-600049-4 (pbk).

The trend toward specialization in science, as well as in other disciplines, makes it difficult for scientists and the general public to remain current with research from a general perspective. To combat that, this book seeks to provide an overview of new developments in eight broadly defined disciplines—astronomy, biology, chemistry, computer science, earth sciences, environment, medicine, and physics. Each article focuses on key theories and discoveries for each disciplines and provides background so general readers can gain an understanding of the underlying principles. For example, the chemistry chapter highlights catalysis, designer proteins, new approaches to synthesis, artificial body parts, silicon chemistry, and new developments in materials science. There are no references for additional reading. The index helps locate specific information. This book succeeds in providing a glimpse at selected new developments in science, but will become outdated. (ANS)

1990 Encyclopedia of information systems and services. 10th ed. Ed. by Amy Lucas. New York: Gale; 1990. 2v. $420. ISBN 0-8103-4745-8.

Volume I contains listings for over 4400 US and foreign companies offering information systems and services. Each entry describes what the company does, where they do it, and who they are. The variety of companies involved in the business of information can be surprising. How many people know of the International Road Research and Documentation organization? or the Aerobics Center Longitudinal Study?

Volume II consists entirely of indexes, such as the Master Index to products and services, a personal name index, geographic index, and function indexes. Advertisements for this title report the price as $210 per volume, but clearly either volume would be of limited utility without the other. (DL)

Graduate research: a guide for students in the sciences. 2nd ed. By Robert V. Smith. New York: Plenum Press; 1990. 292p. $24.95. ISBN 0-306-43465-2.

Written for beginning graduate students and their advisors, this practical guidebook addresses many of the issues facing graduate students in the life, natural, physical, and social-behavioral sciences. The challenges of developing and improving research skills, and preparing for professional careers are the book's primary foci. The author supplies many concrete tips and suggestions on a variety of topics such as time management, the elements of good writing, obtaining grants, preparing theses and dissertations, and presenting and publishing papers. Especially useful is an overview on how to conduct literature searches. Also included are several thoughtful discussions on related philosophical questions such as the role of ethics in science.

The book does a good job of addressing both the practical and philosophical challenges facing the science graduate student. It also provides a useful appendix of scientific databases as well as up-to-date and pertinent references drawn from a wide variety of sources including government documents, biographies, scientific journals, interviews, and conference proceedings. Recommended for academic science collections and for personal purchase. (LD)

Science and Technology Annual Reference Review 1990. Ed. by H. Robert Malinowsky. Phoenix, AZ; Oryx Press; 1990. 358p. $55.00. ISBN 0-89774-527-2; ISSN 1041-2557.

Consists of reviews of 787 books concerned with science, technology, agriculture and medicine. It is limited to those published in 1988 and 1989, with a few 1987 titles. The term "reference" in the title is interpreted as meaning the usual concept, such as handbooks, atlases, tables and histories. Entries are arranged by subjects, then subdivided by types of formats. There are four indexes: titles, authors or editors, subject and type of library for which best suited. The latter index does not appear to be very useful, since it is so difficult to determine what type of library would be interested in a particular book. Otherwise the book should be of considerable value for collection development; the reviews are sufficiently detailed to allow readers to make selections based on them. Shows improvement in number of entries and style of presentation over the first volume, published in 1989. (EM)

COMPUTER SCIENCE

Artificial intelligence terminology: a reference guide. (Ellis Horwood Series in artificial intelligence.) Ed. by Colin Beardon. Chichester: Ellis Horwood Ltd.; 1989. 283p. $67.00. ISBN 0-74580-718-6. $25.00 (pbk). ISBN 0-74580-763-1.

This guide delivers a lot of information very compactly. It will lead the person who is unfamiliar with the jargon of artificial intelligence (AI) to other relevant literature and will place terms in the context of usage and significance within AI disciplines. The editors have selected terms that are well established in AI but that might present problems for anyone approaching AI from another field. Many entries are proper names of significant AI projects that formed the bases for subsequent work. Entries contain words or phrases in brackets that place terms in their usual AI contexts, followed by descriptions of the terms within those contexts. Words or phrases defined elsewhere in the book are italicized. "See also" references guide readers to other related terms. The editors have frequently supplied references to standard works for further reading, and they have included in the introduction a list of general references for each of the major disciplines contributing to the AI field. Highly recommended for academic, technical and large public libraries. (DJR)

NeuralSource: the bibliographic guide to artificial neural networks. Ed. by Philip D. Wasserman and Roberta M. Oetzel. New York: Van Nostrand Reinhold; 1990. 1014p. $65.00.

The literature of artificial neural networks has exploded in the last few years. A retrospective, comprehensive bibliography is essential to anyone entering this interdisciplinary field. Generated from a computerized database, also available for purchase, this book is a handy, economical resource. Periodic updates to the book are planned. *NeuralSource* has a Reference section containing over 4,200 entries in chronological order by year of publication, and in alphabetical order by first author within a given year. Each entry provides full bibliographic information and over 3,000 contain abstracts. Separate author, publication, and keyword indexes enhance access to the references. Highly recommended for academic, technical and large public libraries. (DJR)

EARTH SCIENCES

Dictionary of the environment. 3rd edition. By Michael Allaby. New York: New York University Press; 1989. 423p. $55.00. ISBN 081470591X.

The second edition of the *Dictionary of the environment* has been revised. This updated edition includes many new terms which have become salient as a result of the growth of environmental research, its applications, and the current popular interest in ecological issues. The terms are primarily drawn from the vocabularies of biology and geoscience, but also from chemistry agriculture, nuclear power engineering, and biotechnology. There are individual entries for major environmental disasters, such as the accident at Chernobyl, as well as entries for prominent environmental organizations and activists. This dictionary is useful to a broad audience of users at all levels of sophistication. It would be a worthwhile addition to college, public, and science libraries' collections. (KMK)

Encyclopedia of minerals. 2nd ed. By Willard Lincoln Roberts, Thomas J. Campbell, and George Robert Rapp, Jr. New York: Van Nostrand Reinhold; 1990. 979p. $99.75. ISBN 0-442-27681-8.

Intended for students as well as amateur and professional mineralogists, this comprehensive encyclopedia is an excellent reference source for mineralogical data. Instead of the descriptive articles found in most encyclopedias, this text presents a brief list of factual data for each mineral including chemical formula, crystal system, class, space group, lattice constants, strongest diffraction lines, optical constants, hardness, density, cleavage, habit, and color-luster. Entries also list each mineral's "mode of occurrence" (i.e., the locale where the mineral is most likely to be found). Following each species is a brief but useful list of selected references.

In this second edition, much of the original data was revised and information on over 400 more species was added. Also included are a glossary and more than 300 new black-and-white and color photographs. Although lacking a subject index, the alphabetical arrangement of entries makes this encyclopedia relatively straight-forward and easy to use. Highly recommended for public and academic libraries with mineralogy collections. Should also prove a useful desktop reference for personal collections. (LD)

Information sources in the earth sciences. 2nd ed. Ed. by David N. Wood, Jean E. Hardy, and Anthony P. Harvey. Bowker-Saur; London: Butterworths; 1989. 480p. $85.00. ISBN 0-408-01406-7.

This 1989 compilation, which updates the 1973 edition, is a welcome addition to the field. It provides an up-to-date, comprehensive list of sources that earth scientists should be familiar with. The sources include texts, monographs, reference books, treatises, book series, review publications, and journals for major topics and specific subdisciplines. These major topics include: stratigraphy and regional geology, paleontology, mineralogy and crystallography, geochemistry, petrology, structural geology and tectonics, geophysics, economic geology, engineering and environmental geology, geomorphology and hydrology, meteorology, climatology and soil science. The chapter on maps includes an extensive listing of the most important maps and map series by country. The chapter on computer searching has only five pages of text, but a comprehensive list of databases and databanks worldwide that include information of interest to earth scientists. Each entry includes name of producer and online host, coverage, and file size. The text is a superficial introduction to computer searching and online hosts. As is true for the chapters on secondary literature, little attempt is made to demonstrate how to conduct searches and no footnotes lead the reader to sources that provide the "how to use" or "how to teach use" of the sources. The secondary source chapters focus on descriptive information about the sources. All but one contributor is British and most are geologists. The 1981 edition of *Geologic Reference Sources* by Dederick Ward, Marjorie Wheeler, and Robert Bier is still valuable for its often more detailed list of sources, but the current up-to-date book is essential for all libraries that serve earth scientists. (ANS)

Modern Jeweler's consumer guide to colored gemstones. By David Federman. New York: Van Nostrand Reinhold; 1990. 253p. $19.95. ISBN 0-442-00153-3.

Directed towards average consumers rather than industry specialists, this up-to-date guide profiles sixty of the world's most popular colored gemstones. For each stone reviewed, a brilliant color plate accompanies a 3-page article outlining the geopolitical situation of the supplier country and the gem's present market. Information on common "legitimate" and "illegitimate" enhancements performed on gems as well as suggestions for proper care and handling are also included.

The text is not as detailed or technical as other guides such as *Gem Identification Made Easy* (GemStone Press, 1989). With its paperback format and easy-to-read gem profiles, this book is a good candidate for personal collections. Public libraries with gemology collections should also find it a useful reference source. (LD)

The oceans: a book of questions and answers. By Don Groves. New York: Wiley; 1989. 203p. $12.95. ISBN 0-471-60712-6.

Presented in a readable question-and-answer format, this introductory level guide supplies numerous facts and figures on the world's oceans. In writing this book the author hoped to better educate the average layperson in order to ensure continued public interest in ocean science and engineering. The text itself is organized into 50 major sections covering the ocean's physical, biological, meteorological, chemical, and geological characteristics respectively. A separate section explores some of the challenges of ocean engineering such as marine fouling.

The last chapter contains a hodgepodge of information answering a wide variety of general interest questions (e.g., What is Atlantis? Who invented the first submarine? What is the U.S. National Ocean Service?). Completing the text are a brief glossary of terms and a fairly good general bibliography listing various textbooks, journal articles, and government reports for more in-depth reading. A subject index is also included. Requiring no scientific/technical background of its audience, this guidebook would be most appropriate for high school and public libraries as well as personal collections. (LD)

The water encyclopedia. 2nd ed. Ed. by Frits van der Leeden et al. Chelsea, Michigan: Lewis Publishers; 1990. 808p. $125.00. ISBN 0-0-87371-120-3.

Revised and expanded since the 1970 edition, the Encyclopedia is a vast compilation of data useful to hydrologists, engineers, irrigation specialists, hydrogeologists, environmentalists and developers of public policy. It reprints more than 600 tables and 100 illustrations, each with source noted (U.S.G.S., E.P.A., A.W.W.A., Statistical Abstracts of the U.S., etc.). Chapter titles: climate and precipitation, hydrologic elements, surface water, ground water, water use, water quality, environmental problems, water resource management, water laws and treaties, agencies and organizations, consultants and conversion factors. Keep this book near the reference desk! (IK)

ENGINEERING AND TECHNOLOGY

Battery reference book. By T. R. Crompton. Boston: Butterworths; 1990. Various pagination. $150.00. ISBN 0-408-00790-7.

This practical handbook successfully synthesizes a wealth of information on all types of commercially produced batteries. Both primary (non-rechargeable) and secondary (rechargeable) batteries ranging in size from pacemaker batteries to aircraft batteries are covered. The text begins with a chapter on the basic theory behind the operation of batteries, later addressing a wide variety of topics including design, performance characteristics, applications, and charging.

The text contains some useful special features including an appendix of battery standards; a list of battery journals, trade organizations, and conferences; and the names and addresses of primary and secondary battery suppliers worldwide. Other standard features such as a glossary, a brief bibliography, and a subject index are also provided. By drawing together a variety of practical information in one source, this comprehensive handbook will be a useful desk reference for battery manufacturers, electronic and electrical engineers, and designers of battery powered equipment. (LD)

Biomass handbook. Ed. by Osamu Kitani, Carl W. Hall et al. New York: Gordon and Breach; 1989. 963p. $349.00. ISBN 2-88124-269-3.

Biochemists, chemical engineers and environmentalists will find much to "digest" in this major work on plant and animal product utilization. It contains about 100 very readable articles (most are under ten pages) with tables, diagrams and extensive bibliographies on topics pertaining to biomass production, biomass conversion, biomass utilization, biotechnology for biomass, and biomass statistics and properties. Here is a sampling of articles: global circulation of carbon, forestry products and waste, seaweeds, methane fermentation, amylase, dehydration, densification, root crops, vegetable oils for engine fuels, economics of biomass systems, bioelectric cells. There are author and subject indexes. Contributors are primarily from universities and research institutes, many from Japan. Recommended for all technical libraries. (IK)

The C4 handbook: CAD, CAM, CAE, CIM. (Computer graphics technology and management series.) Ed. by Carl Machover. Blue Ridge Summit, PA: Tab Books Inc.; 1989. 438p. $44.50. ISBN 0-8306-9398-X.

This is a revised edition of the author's 1980 book: The CAD/CAM Handbook. The dramatic growth in this industry is evidenced by the need to expand the title to include CAE (Computer Aided Engineering) and the CIM (Computer Integrated Manufacturing).

This handbook is geared more for the industry executive or manager than for the engineer. It gives a general overview of these quickly changing fields complete with a glossary of terms, a small bibliography of current books and important journals and newsletters, and an index. It is a very readable book. Most chapters are on different workstation applications; each gives a brief history, current trends and future developments.

This book will be very useful to the student doing research in this area and for the executive who needs information for planning and the terminology to intelligently talk to engineers. Highly recommended for all college libraries. (RK)

Chemical engineering faculties, 1989-1990. Ed. by James B. Rawlings. New York: American Institute of Chemical Engineers; 1989. 196p. $40.00. ISBN 0-8169-0467-7.

AIChE's annual listing of chemical engineering faculties is organized by country, with U.S. entries subdivided by state. Data include address, phone, FAX and electronic mail address, accreditation status, AIChE student chapter information, degrees granted, contact person in graduate admissions, listing of department faculty and rank. There is an alphabetical index of faculty names for U.S. and Canadian schools and a listing of Omega Chi Epsilon chapters. Unlike the *ACS Directory of Graduate Research*, the work has no information on fields of current research. The ASEE journal, *Engineering Education*, provides more in-depth data on engineering programs including chemical engineering, but does not include faculty names. (IK)

Datapro manufacturing automation series. By Datapro Research. NJ: McGraw-Hill; 1987- $884.

The Manufacturing Automation Series is one of a number of well-done loose-leaf publications written by Datapro Research. Others include: information processing, microcomputers, office automation, communications, and industry automation. These series are noted for being up-to-date, concise, well written and fairly comprehensive in coverage. Depending upon the series and the volume, each is updated every month or two.

The Manufacturing Automation Series is divided into five loose-leaf folders: News and Perspectives; Manufacturing and Planning; Manufacturing Information systems; CAD/CAM/CAE Systems; and Factory Automation Systems. Each of the three systems volumes will devote chapters describing the major computer systems on the market, giving specifications, prices, analysis and comparative information. The News and Perspective volume consists of a monthly report covering industry trends, related news items or major product announcements. The Management and Planning volume covers strategies for implementing these automated systems. Each volume has its own index.

The information in this series can be found in other publications, but what makes Datapro fairly unique is their ability to pull this large amount of information together. Another company that produces similar loose-leaf style publications covering many aspects of automation is Faulkner Technical Reports. Both companies are willing to send their publications to you for review. I would recommend doing this for comparison before making a commitment to purchase. Datapro Manufacturing Automation Series is recommended for libraries whose companies are involved in the research or purchase of manufacturing systems and for large academic libraries who support both engineering and management programs. (RK)

Directory of testing laboratories, 1989 edition. Compiled by ASTM. Philadelphia: ASTM; 1989. 299p. $50.00. ISBN 0-8031-1212-2; ISSN 0895-7886.

Testing laboratories in the U.S., Canada and 29 other countries are represented. Geographic, alphabetic and subject indexes guide the user to entries which include company name, address, phone, contact person, specialties, fields of testing (i.e., acoustic, chemical, geotechnical, radiation, etc.), types of materials and products tested (i.e., agricultural, fibers, machinery, metals, construction, etc.), descriptions of equipment used for tests, staff size and level, and locations of branch offices. Although compiled by ASTM, they repeatedly note a disclaimer that the work is not intended, nor should be used, as a listing of ASTM certified labs. (IK)

Eshbach's handbook of engineering fundamentals. 4th ed. Ed. by Byron D. Tapley, NY: Wiley; 1990. Various pagination. $64.95. ISBN 0-47189-084-7.

This handbook is designed as a quick desk reference for practicing engineers and advanced students. The coverage is broad enough to cover most engineering disciplines yet detailed enough to answer specific questions. Besides engineering principles, the handbook also contains chapters on units of measure. It is fairly unique in that there really isn't a similar book on the market since most handbooks are geared towards specific disciplines such as Marks' Standard Handbook for Mechanical Engineers or Perry's Chemical Engineers Handbook. Eshbach's Handbook is well illustrated with graphs, charts, tables and formulas. The index is adequate but could utilize more cross references.

This reasonably priced handbook is a worth while addition for all academic engineering reference collections. (RK)

Handbook of HVAC design. Ed. by Nils R. Grimm and Robert C. Rosaler. New York: McGraw-Hill; 1990. Various pagination. $96.00. ISBN 0-07-024841-9.

With contributions by more than 30 experts in the field, this guide addresses the planning, design, equipment selection, operation, and maintenance of heating, ventilation, and air conditioning systems. It details the uses, operational features, and performance characteristics of various HVAC systems including heating equipment and distribution systems, cooling systems, cogeneration systems, pumps, valves and water conditioning components. In addition, mechanical and automated environmental control systems for maintaining temperature and humidity are covered.

While the topics addressed herein are similar to those covered in the multi-volume *ASHRAE Handbook*, the text in hand does not duplicate the ASHRAE work which is significantly more detailed. Recommended for technical collections supporting the design, construction, and operation of residential, commercial, and industrial buildings. Useful chapter references as well as numerous illustrations and a substantial subject index are included. (LD)

Handbook of plastics test methods. 3rd ed. Ed. by Roger P. Brown. Essex, England: Longman Scientific & Technical Ltd.; New York: Wiley; in conjunction with The Plastics and Rubber Institute; 1989. 592p. $159.00. ISBN 0-470-21134-2.

This new edition (2nd edition, 1981) presents up-to-date procedures for physical testing methods and seeks to be comprehensive in covering national and international procedures. The international (ISO) standards are emphasized, along with standards from Britain, United States (ASTM), and Germany (DIN) which are the most frequently referenced national standards. Chapters cover preparation of test pieces and test atmospheres. Other chapters cover testing for: density; stress-strain; friction and wear; creep and relaxation; electrical, optical, and thermal properties; effect of temperature; environmental resistance; fire testing; non-destructive testing; and permeability. Each chapter ends with an extensive bibliography. An excellent handbook for libraries serving plastics engineers. (ANS)

Handbook of utilities and services for buildings: planning, design, and installation. Edited by Cyril M. Harris. New York: McGraw-Hill; 1990. Various pagination. $74.50. ISBN 0-07-026829-0.

Addressed to architects, engineers, contractors, and other technical professionals, this practical handbook explores the design, specification, and installation of utilities and services for commercial, industrial, and multi-residential buildings. A variety of basic services such as water supply, drainage, refuse disposal, gas supply, electrical supply, telecommunications, and building security are covered in-depth. On the other hand, janitorial and maintenance services as well as environmental control services (e.g., air conditioning, lighting, etc.) are excluded altogether.

To its credit, this book addresses technical information in a fairly accessible manner with numerous charts and diagrams further clarifying the text. An adequate subject index and limited chapter references are also included. Should prove a useful addition to any technical collection in building construction. (LD)

Information sources in polymers and plastics. Ed. by R.T. Adkins. London: Bowker-Saur Ltd.; 1989. 313p. $75.00. ISBN 0-408-02027-X.

The book offers an extensive discussion and listing of information sources in polymers and plastics. The first group of chapters cover: journals; abstract and index publications; books, encyclopedias, and reviews; patents and trademarks; standards; trade literature, theses, and conferences; and online data bases. An extensive list of data bases and property data banks notes publisher, host systems, file size, and descriptive comment. The second group of chapters covers sources by type of information provided, e.g., nomenclature, properties, business information; fibers, etc. The third group describes sources specific to geographic areas, e.g., Europe, Americas, Japan, and Pacific Basin, along with translation titles. The only similar source of polymer literature published in the last ten years appeared in volume 9 of *Encyclopedia of Polymer Science and Engineering* (2nd edition, 1987, p. 62-97). In some cases the *Encyclopedia*'s list of sources is more extensive, while in most areas the Adkins book covers the topic in greater detail. Most chapters have been written by information specialists. A necessary book for all libraries serving polymer and plastics students and researchers. (ANS)

Pump Applications Desk Book. By Paul N. Garay. Englewood Cliffs, NJ: Prentice-Hall; 1990. 300p. $56.00. ISBN 0-88173-043-2 Text Ed.

This handbook provides guidelines for selecting the optimum pump for engineering applications. It describes the various modes of operation, potential configurations for various applications, limitations for specific types of pumps, and the effect of design on economy and reliability. An excellent summary and reference book for engineering pump applications. (ANS)

1990 SAE Handbook. Ed. by the Cooperative Engineering Program. Warrendale, PA: Society of Automotive Engineers, Inc.; 1990. 4 vols. $175.00. ISBN 0-89883-891-6.

Automotive engineering is a very broad based discipline requiring expertise in mechanical, electrical and materials engineering. Because of this, information in this handbook will be of importance to a wide engineering audience.

The *SAE Handbook* is an annual publication that contains technical reports written by the Society of Automotive Engineers. These reports include mostly SAE standards plus recommended practices and information reports. Even though each volume of this 4 volume set can be purchased individually, I would recommend purchasing the entire set in order to provide your readers with a complete collection of all SAE standards. Volume

1 deals with Materials; volume 2 with Parts and Components; volume 3 with Engines, Fuels, Lubricants, Emissions and Noise; and volume 4 contains reports on On-Highway Vehicles and Off-Highway Machinery. Each volume is divided into three main sections: a numerical index, a subject index and the actual technical reports.

Most of the information contained in this handbook can also be found in the comprehensive microfilm collection of standards produced by either Information Handling Services or the National Standards Association. If your library does not have access to these collections, then the *SAE Handbook* would be a good addition. I would highly recommend this book to libraries requiring a comprehensive reference collection on automotive engineering. (RK)

Standards, a resource and guide for identification, selection, and acquisition. By Patricia L. Ricci and Linda Perry. St. Paul: Stirtz, Bernards and Company; 1990. 239p. $60.00.

The introduction states that ". . . this book was created to provide answers to the most common standards questions asked by the average user . . ." To that end it contains information on standards-producing agencies in the U.S. and abroad; libraries and information centers; union lists, vendors, consultants, conferences, courses and newsletters relating to standards; a bibliography of standards resources; a list of former names of organizations and a list of alphabetic designations used by standards agencies. Information was garnered from responses to questionnaires. Some entries are incomplete, presumably because data was not supplied by the respondents. But other gaps exist (i.e., only four libraries are listed for New York State), the more frustrating for lack of explanation by the authors. How were the libraries chosen? If there is no indication of holdings, is it assumed the libraries have a complete set of standards for the agencies listed? What is meant when an organization is characterized as having an "obsolete collection?" Unless your library collects everything on standards you can probably rely on more familiar sources like the *Encyclopedia of Associations, Yearbook of International Organizations, Index and Directory of U.S. Industry Standards* and the ANSI catalog to answer questions by the average user. (IK)

Comment from Author Received by EDITOR

In response to the reviewers question: "how were the libraries chosen?", we wrote to the worldwide members of International Association of University Technical Libraries and public libraries in the 250 largest U.S. cities. The one half responded and their responses varied greatly in completeness but were used as received. Information on additional public-access standards collections was also extracted from several local union lists of standards. In spite of the inconsistent information, the library information is useful as a starting point in one's local community. Obsolete collection means the library keeps issues of standards which have been superseded. This information is useful in litigation. The *Encyclopedia of Associations* and the *Yearbook of International Organizations* together do not contain all the standards writing organizations. The *IHS Index and Directory of U.S. Industry Standards* costs 4 times as much and its indexing is a good complement to the information in my book on courses, vendors, union lists, consultants, reference resources, databases and alpha designations of standards. Stirtz Bernards is no longer distributing this book and it is available directly from Patricia Ricci, 8590 S. Pinehurst Alcove, Woodbury, MN 55125. Prepayment is required.

Patricia Ricci

HEALTH SCIENCES

Handbook of normal physical measurements. By Judith G. Hall, Ursula G. Froster-Iskenius and Judith E. Allanson. New York: Oxford Press; 1989. 504p. $75. ISBN 0-19-261696-X.

What is normal? This guide gives a series of age-related norms, comparative values for different parts of the body, and comparative values for different points in a patient's life. Most parents are familiar with height (or length) and weight tables for infants which relate weight to height and both values to age. This book attempts to provide the same data for other body size parameters.

For each value, the authors describe the method used for taking measurements, provide growth charts culled from the literature, and cite references to aid in understanding the statistics.

The authors intend to help health professionals better define congenital anomalies and syndromes by presenting them with a range of values which can be used to define "normal." (DL)

A Bibliography of medical and biomedical biography. By Leslie T. Morton and Robert J. Moore. Brookfield, VT: Gower; 1989. 208p. $69.95. ISBN 0-85967-797-4.

The biographies cited are limited to English-language profiles of more than 2000 health professionals, biochemists, biophysicists, physiologists, pharmacologists, and geneticists. The body of the work is arranged alphabetically by biographee. Each entry gives the subject's profession and dates of birth and death. Citations to published and unpublished biographies follow the brief biographical information. An index by discipline is provided. (DL)

Health care standards 1990 official directory. Plymouth Meeting, PA: ECRI; 1990. 814p. $245. ISBN 0-941417-15-8.

Described by the title as a directory of organizations that have issued health care standards, this publication serves even more usefully as a bibliography of citations to published standards, legislation, and journal articles.

The first major section consists of an alphabetical list of organizations. The name, address and phone number of an organization are followed by references to whatever health care standards that organization has authored, and the year each standard was produced. The second section of the book reports legislative standards. The entries are arranged by federal agency, and by state and keyword within state.

An extensive keyword index provides subject access to organizational and legislative standards. Since the book contains only citations, not the standards themselves, libraries will have to have access to the countless different publications which contain these standards. Still, it's a place to start. (DL)

Drug-test interactions handbook. Edited by J.G. Salway. New York: Raven; 1990. 1087p. $320. ISBN 0-88167-602-0.

Picture a severely ill patient, currently taking an assortment of drugs, either to alleviate pain or to cure disease. If a physician performs a series of tests on that patient, will the test results match the results of the same tests performed on a healthy individual? Probably not. But is the difference due to the patient's illness, or to one or more of the drugs he's taking?

This book attempts to answer those kinds of questions. It lists over 12,000 drug-test interactions. Two types of interactions are reported. Biological interactions arise because the drug being taken affects the body's ability to produce the substance being measured by the test. Tegretol does inhibit the body's production of calcium, so patients who take Tegretol will show lower calcium levels. On the other hand, patients who use toothpaste before a saliva test for progesterone will show higher levels of that hormone because toothpaste interferes with the saliva test. This is called analytical interference.

Researchers attempt to correct for these effects by designing experiments which include control subjects. Consulting this reference would familiarize them with all sources interference and allow them to plan even better controls. Readers of scientific articles would also find this book useful in evaluating the methods used in experiments. (DL)

A basic guide to online information systems for health care professionals. By Ronald G. Albright. Arlington, VA: Information Resource Press; 1988. 296p. $27.50. ISBN 0-87815-056-0.

Written for physicians and other health care professionals who wish to do their own online searching for topics in the health sciences. Chapters are devoted to health care information from the practitioner's viewpoint, online resources from the National Library of Medicine, CompuServe, Paper-Chase, Dialog and Knowledge Index, BRS/Colleague, MEDIS, AMA/ NET, how systems work, and selection of modems and communications software. Appendixes include such topics as use of Boolean logic and system vendors. Provides adequate information for those willing to follow its pathway through the thicket of online sources. The author is himself an M.D. (EM)

Directory of biomedical and health care grants 1988-1990. 4th ed. Phoenix, AZ: Oryx Press; 1989. 571p. $74.50. ISSN 0883333-5330.

A thorough index of more than 3000 research programs related to health care. They range from strictly laboratory projects to those involving health care delivery. Although it concentrates on the United States and Canada, other countries are included also. Each description indicates the nature of the programs, amount of grant money available, dates of applications and renewal dates, sponsoring organization and person to contact. There is a subject index as well as two for sponsoring organizations, one arranged by type and another arranged alphabetically. (EM)

The sourcebook of medical illustration. Ed. by Peter Cull. New Jersey: Parthenon; 1989. 481p. $65.00. ISBN 0-940813-72-6.

The authors of this collection of over 500 line drawings state in their introduction that the drawings may be copied and used freely. They ask only that the source of the illustration be acknowledged. This resource is intended for health care workers and scientists who wish to produce slides, posters, video, or other illustrated publications, but who do not have a graphic artist at their beck and call. Diagrams cover: body outlines; bones and joints; heart, lungs and circulation; digestive tract; liver, gall bladder, pancreas, and spleen; kidneys and bladder; female and male genital tracts; brain and nervous system; endocrine and ductless glands; eye, ear, nose, and throat; skin; obstetrics; cells and tissues; anaesthesia; bacteria; yeasts; protozoans and viruses; medical symbols and animals; map of countries throughout the world; and various kinds of lettering. (DL)

LIFE SCIENCES

A Dictionary of ethology. (Worterbuch der verhaltensforschung. English.) By Klau Immelmann and Colin Beer. Cambridge, Mass.: Harvard University Press; 1989. 336p. $36.00. ISBN 0-674-20506-5.

This is a new version of Immelmann's *Dictionary of Ethological Terms* which was published in German in 1975. The dictionary contains definitions of ethological, physiological and sociobiological terms and phrases. Some of the entries, such as the definitions of enzymes, are a few words long. Others, involving concepts or paradigms, are essays that are several pages long. The essays explain the term and its significance in ethology. In addition some of the longer entries included give the history of particular concepts and the current status of related research. Most of the material in the volume will be familiar to working ethologists and sociobiologists. The book is likely to be more useful to students and researchers in related fields than it will be to ethologists. This dictionary is an appropriate addition to life sciences or comprehensive science collections. (KMK)

Dictionary of immunology. By Fred S. Rosen, Linda S. Steiner and Emil R. Unanue. New York: Stockton Press; 1989. 223p. $50.00. ISBN 0-935859-58-6.

Approximately 1200 words and phrases used in immunology, cell biology, molecular biology, and genetics are included. Immunologists will already know most of these terms. After all, they invented them. But students and professionals in other fields will find this dictionary useful. Conversely, immunologists would benefit from the genetics or molecular and cell biology perspectives included in the definitions. (DL)

Foundations of laboratory safety: a guide for the biomedical laboratory. By Stephen R. Rayburn. New York: Springer Verlag; 1990. 418p. $59.00. ISBN 0-387-97125-4.

This is a comprehensive text on biomedical laboratory safety. Rayburn has included material on all the fundamental hazards and safety procedures for workers who handle biological agents, chemicals and radioisotopes. This volume is something more than a safety manual — it is suitable for use as textbook, as well. The author has provided an extensive list of references to the material in each chapter. There is also a bibliography for further readings which is organized by subject. This guide is well organized and well written, and will be useful to all biomedical laboratory personnel — researchers, students and staff. (KMK)

Grzimek's Encyclopedia of Mammals. (Grzimek's Enzyklopadie Saugetiere. English.) Ed. by Bernhard Grzimek. New York: McGraw-Hill; 1990. 5 vol. $500.00. ISBN 0079095089.

Grzimek's Encyclopedia of Mammals is an updated, revised and expanded edition of the mammalian section of Grzimek's well known *Animal Life Encyclopedia*. That work has been greatly expanded and it incorporates the new data and increased understanding generated by the past fifteen years' research in biology, conservation and ethology.

The encyclopedia includes a wealth of information on the diverse forms of mammalian life. The work is organized taxonomically by orders and families. Each section includes information on evolution, phylogeny, anatomy, physiology, ecophysiology, ecology, ethology, paleontology, conservation and endangerment. Typical and atypical genus and species are used as exemplars within the family sections. Summary tables and graphs have been included which help the reader grasp the similarities and differences between related species. The geographical distribution maps in this edition are larger and more readable than those in the earlier work. The encyclopedia is lavishly illustrated with full and double page color photographs. Many of these are "action photographs" of animals engaged in predation, feeding, or movement. Morphological features such as dentition, skeletal anatomy, and facial conformation are illustrated by sketches and photographs. As in the older edition, individual species are depicted in color drawings.

There are numerous animal encyclopediae, and several devoted to mammals. None of the others compare with Grzimek's new work. This is the best reference work on mammals and the only one which is comprehensive. (KMK)

Handbook of biological illustration. 2nd ed. (Chicago guides to writing, editing and publishing.) By Frances W. Zweifel. Chicago: University of Chicago Press; 1988. 160p. $27.00 (hardcover). ISBN 02-226-99700-6; $9.95 (pbk). ISBN 0-226-99701-4.

This small handbook, written by a free-lance biological illustrator serves as an introduction to biological illustrations. Chapters cover size of drawings, materials, completing the drawing and lettering, and preparing graphs, maps, photographs, plates, and projection slides. The emphasis is on hand work rather than computer graphics. This handbook, which focuses on artistic illustration can be a helpful companion to *Illustrating Science: Standards for Publication* (prepared by the Council of Biology Editors, Bethesda, MD, 1988), which aims to develop standards and guidelines for publication of illustrated scientific materials. (ANS)

Principal diseases of marine fish and shellfish. Vol. 1. 2nd ed. By Carl J. Sindermann. San Diego, CA: Academic Press; 1989. $89.00. ISBN 0-12-645-851-0.

This is the first of two volumes which update the 1970 edition of Sindermann's book. This volume is devoted to infectious and noninfectious fish diseases and the second volume will cover shellfish diseases. The most common diseases caused by bacteria, viruses, protozoa, helminths and fungi, as well as neoplastic diseases, genetic disorders and environmentally related conditions are covered. All the first species that are mentioned in the volume are either commonly kept as captive populations or are economically significant marine populations. The author has included a wealth of references for primary sources on fish pathologies. A subject index lists the first and the pathogens by their genus and species, and also includes disease names, classes of disease and some general concepts. Judged as a reference book, the volume's only shortcoming is that it is not comprehensive with regard to fish diseases or fish populations. This volume would be most useful to marine biologists, marine aquaculturists; and fishery scientists. (KMK)

Writing papers in the biological sciences. By Victoria E. McMillan. New York: St. Martin's Press; 1988. 150p. ISBN 0-312-89489-9.

This valuable book is aimed at helping undergraduate students learn to write biological research papers, although graduate students will also find this information helpful. The author discusses: each part of a paper (title, abstract, introduction, methodology, results, discussion, tables and figures, references), drafting and writing. Writing hints (punctuation, verb tense, etc.), names of organisms, and symbols and abbreviations are covered. In many cases examples of well executed writing is presented, often with comparisons to less effective versions. The book is written in a clear, understandable, and unintimidating style. The bibliography of additional readings includes other guides to scientific writing, including the standard *CBE Style Manual* from the Council of Biology Editors. An essential book for all academic and medium-large public libraries. (ANS)

PHYSICAL SCIENCES

4-Aminobenzenesulfonamides. (International Union of Pure & Applied Chemistry, Solubility Data Series, vols. 34-36). Ed. by Anthony N. Paruta and Ryszard Piekos. Oxford, New York: Pergamon Press; 1988-89. 3 vols. 372p. $120.00. ISBN 0-08-030742-6 (v.34). 369p. $120.00. ISBN 0-08-034708-8 (v.35). 552p. $120.00. ISBN 0-08-034710-X (v.36).

Another set of volumes in the IUPAC Solubility Data Series that compactly compiles and critically evaluates solubility data for sulfanilamide and its derivatives. The substances are divided into three volumes according to structure: non-cyclic; 5-membered heterocycles, and 6-membered heterocycles. The evaluation process is defined in general and for each system. Evaluated solubility data for a wide variety of aqueous, organic, and inorganic solvents is provided, along with references to relevant journal articles. Indexes covering substance name, Chemical Abstracts Service Registry Number, and author of referenced articles appear in each volume, but there is no cumulative index. Useful for academic research libraries serving chemists. (ANS)

Comprehensive organic transformations: a guide to functional group preparations. By Richard C. Larock. New York: VCH; 1989. 1100p. $55.00. ISBN 0-89573-710-8.

This compilation provides a comprehensive, highly condensed, systematic collection of 15,000 reactions used in organic synthesis. The reactions are arranged according to functional group being synthesized and subdivided into major reactions, such as oxidation, reduction, alkylation, etc. The detailed table-of-contents provides easy access to information. In addition, a unique Transformation Index that lists, in the first column, the organic product of the transformation and, in the second column, the organic starting material along with the page that describes the transformation. For each reaction, the general reaction, reagents, reaction conditions, and selected references are provided. Literature coverage is complete through 1987. This compact compilation will be indispensable for all synthetic chemists and all libraries serving them. (ANS)

The chemist's ready reference handbook. By Gershon J. Shugar and John A. Dean. New York: McGraw-Hill; 1990. 640p. $89.50. ISBN 0-07057-178-3.

This excellent handbook aims to provide practical information needed for laboratory experiments by chemists, both as students and on-the-job. It provides up-to-date instructions, guidelines, and practical checklists with troubleshooting hints for common experimental techniques. It updates and extends, on a brief and more technical level, information contained in the 1981 *Chemical Technicians' Ready Reference Handbook*. Chapters cover newer techniques, such as High Performance Liquid Chromatography. The focus is on equipment and procedures, in contrast to the *Chemists' Companion* (Wiley, 1972) which provides typical results and data determined from the experiments in addition to briefer descriptions of equipment and procedures. Two practical chapters cover preparation of solutions and determination of physical properties, such as density, viscosity, surface tension, optical rotation, and refractive index. Each chapter ends with a list of recent, selected references. Essential for all libraries serving chemists. (ANS)

Comprehensive organic transformations: a guide to functional group preparations. By Richard C. Larock. New York: VCH; 1989. 1100p. $55.00. ISBN 0-89573-710-8.

This compilation provides a comprehensive, highly condensed, systematic collection of 15,000 reactions used in organic synthesis. The reactions are arranged according to functional group being synthesized and subdivided into major reactions, such as oxidation, reduction, alkylation, etc. The detailed table-of-contents provides easy access to information. In addition, a unique Transformation Index that lists, in the first column, the organic product of the transformation and, in the second column, the organic starting material along with the page that describes the transformation. For each reaction, the general reaction, reagents, reaction conditions, and selected references are provided. Literature coverage is complete through 1987. This compact compilation will be indispensable for all synthetic chemists and all libraries serving them. (ANS)

Dictionary of chemistry and chemical technology: English-German. 4th ed. Helmut Gross, Editor-in-Chief. New York: Elsevier, 1989. 752p. $150.00. ISBN 0-44498-863-7.

This fourth edition contains 60,000 terms, including new terms from analytical chemistry, kinetics, biochemistry, biotechnology, hydrochemistry, and food technology. This dictionary, which provides the German equivalent for English terms, is the companion to the 1984 volume that converts German terms into English. A special value of the present volume is to help utilize German journals and such reference sources as Beilstein, which is now available in English since the fifth Supplement and in its computerized format. The 1979, second revised edition of L. DeVries and H. Kolb's *Dictionary of Chemistry and Chemical Engineering* (Verlag Chemie) is sometimes more complete. If more recent terminology is needed, the Helmut Gross volume would be helpful. (ANS)

Polymer science dictionary. By Mark S.M. Alger. New York: Elsevier Science Publishers; 1989. 532p. $176.50. ISBN 1-85166-220-0.

The *Dictionary* includes more than 6000 entries for materials, processes, properties and mathematical expressions relevant to polymers (including some biopolymers, but excluding the terminology of polymer processing).
    Many of the entries are for trade names. Some are specific, i.e., DELRIN, tradename for polyoxymethylene; others are generic, i.e., DEN, tradename for an epoxy resin. None shows name of manufacturer, so additional research in other sources would be needed to identify or obtain the material. A comparison to tradename coverage between the *Dictionary* and *Encyclopedia of plastics, polymers and resins* (Chemical Publishing Co.,

1982) and *Gardiner's chemical synonyms and tradenames*, 9th ed. (Gower, 1987) is inconclusive. Each title has some entries the other lacks. The latter two, however, give more information for each entry.

The author is at the London School of Polymer Science. He states in the Preface that in compiling this work ". . . about 1000 specialist polymer monographs and numerous reviews have been consulted." The librarian in me wishes a bibliography of at least some of those references had been included. The *Dictionary* is no substitute for encyclopedic works on polymers or for monographs on specific topics, but it has more information on polymers than a general technical dictionary and may be adequate if short explanations will suffice. (IK)

Positrons and positronium: a bibliography 1930-1984. (Physical Sciences Data v.33). Ed. by Y.C. Jean, R.M. Lambrecht, and D. Horvath. Amsterdam, New York: Elsevier; 1988. 1236p. $395.00. ISBN 0-444-43021-0 (v.33).

This bibliography includes articles, proceedings, abstracts, reports and patents published between 1930 and 1984. Topics included are: fundamental properties, interactions with matter, nuclear technology, history and philosophy of antimatter, theory of the universe, and applications of positrons in chemical, physical, and biomedical sciences. The 7700 entries are arranged chronologically by year and in alphabetical order by the first author. Includes an author index. A brief "Principal Subject Index" is slightly helpful in locating articles on a specific topic, but is sufficiently general that 190 articles listed under "Angular Correlation" can be time consuming to follow-up. Considering the cost and difficulty in locating articles on a specific subject, this volume is best suited for research collections serving elementary particle physicists. (ANS)

Thermochemical data of pure substances. By Ihsan Barin. New York: VCH; 1990. 2 vols. 816p. $407.00. ISBN 3-527-27812-5 (German). ISBN 0-89573-866-X (U.S.).

Eight major thermodynamic properties are listed for 2400 substances as a function of temperature at 100 degree intervals. These 2400 substances, the most comprehensive single listing, covers the elements and compounds of 2-4 elements. Most substances are inorganic, but some hydrocarbons and carbohydrates are included. The data largely came from sources of critically evaluated data such as the JANAF Tables and compilations by the U.S. Bureau of Mines, as well as journal articles and other compilations. An index by molecular formula aids rapid location of a substance. Essential for libraries that serve chemists, metallurgists, material scientists, and ceramic and chemical engineers. (ANS)

SCI-TECH IN REVIEW

Karla J. Pearce, Editor

ONLY READ WHAT YOU FIND INTERESTING

Aldridge, Susan. How to cut a swathe through the literature. *New Scientist*. 125(1707): 69; 10 March 1990.

Applying the 80/20 rule to their choice of reading will alleviate scientists' guilt for not reading everything in their field. It has been demonstrated, after all, that performing 20% of a task will yield an 80% result. One can choose to read journals listed in just two sections of the ten represented in Current Contents, then opt to scan only 20 of these titles. Reading "Citation Classics" and the quarterly listings of most highly cited papers from *Science Citation Index* will give one an idea of what s/he might have missed. A light-hearted solution to the stress producing problem of keeping up with the literature.

A LITTLE MORE MODESTY, PLEASE

Beckett, Chris. The great chain of being. *New Scientist*. 125(1709): 66-67; 24 March 1990.

The author, a social worker, comments on the extravagant claims favored by scientists who write for a wide audience. Stephen Hawking writes that the goal of science is to provide "a single theory that describes the whole universe." But while the Grand Unified Theory (GUT) would answer many questions, it would certainly leave the majority unexplained. For most of the human race, GUT would make small difference to their daily lives. Scientific theory is most useful at the molecular level, but beyond that its most useful contribution is its objective approach to problem solving and the useful metaphors it provides. She suggests a little more modesty in science writers' approaches to human problems.

PRESERVING, CATALOGING AND DECODING DATA FROM SPACE

Blakeslee, Sandra. Lost on earth: wealth of data found in space. *New York Times*. Final edition; Section C, 1. 20 March 1990.

If we think it's difficult to keep of track of volumes in a library, consider the problems of collecting, decoding, cataloging and preserving the electronic data sent to earth from NASA missions. It's difficult to know what should be kept, since these data may contain answers to questions that were only asked after they were collected. Recent proof for the thinning of the ozone layer, for example, was found in data that had been gathered in the 1970's but ignored because the readings were so low that they seemed to be in error. Some older tapes could not be read because the source codes to their computer programs had been lost, or the machines which were designed to interpret them became obsolete before the tapes were read, or the coating on old tapes flaked off. Added to the challenge of reading data already on tape is that of what will come in in the future—NASA's "Mission to the Planet Earth" program, in one day, will generate more data than have already been generated by the space program. Scientists at the Jet Propulsion Laboratory, where the tapes are being cataloged, have an enormous assignment ahead of them.

LANS FOR THE SMALL LIBRARY

Howden, Norman. Local area network management: an unresolved issue. *Microcomputers for Information Management*. 6(4): 281-291; 1989 December.

For small libraries that are not automated beyond the occasional microcomputer, a model for planning a LAN network can be very helpful. The author lists the immediate goals and larger objectives for such a model. He describes and evaluates a project that was carried out at the Library School and the Science Library at the University of North Texas. Problems ranged from technical ones which involved choosing cabling and connectors to those with organizational and administrative implications. Management of files and training of new users turned out to be more important than had been anticipated. Finally, we are cautioned not to forget the costs of overhead.

CHOOSING PERIODICALS

Johnston, Wanda K. Periodical selection using weighted criteria cost-benefit analysis. *Library Administration and Management*. 4(2): 96-100; 1990 Spring.

After detailing the milestones along the path to more and more expensive journals, the author suggests criteria that are weighted and used to select and deselect journals in a community college library. The first criterion, usage, covers both circulation and browsing. Relevance, the second, is defined by numbers of titles in which a journal is indexed, numbers of credit hours for associated courses, Katz ratings and includes a bonus for meeting special curricular needs. Fax availability and cost are the other criteria. Using a formula that the author claims allows for the 80/20 rule — 80% of circulation is satisfied by 20% of the library — 46 journals are ranked. McCall's scores the highest while the Journal of American History is 46th. An interesting approach, but I would certainly question the application of the 80/20 rule here.

ENGINEERING STUDENTS
LEARN TO DO LIBRARY RESEARCH

Shoolbred, Michael. Writing a project: a library user education package for engineering students. *Education for Information*. 8: 33-40; 1990.

In the mid-1980's the author noted that there were not enough library staff at the Birmingham Polytechnic to give engineering students the help they needed to conduct their library research efficiently, so that they would produce a polished and professional report. He designed a user education package to meet those needs and tested it on students and colleagues. What finally developed were a series of booklets on the topics of searching the literature, information sources, sources outside the library, how to write it up and a guide to bibliographic references. The package takes an open learning approach, centered on the learner, and has been quite successful with both students and librarians. It is available from the author on paper or on disk for 10 British Pounds, compatible with both IBM-PC or Apple MacIntosh.

JUST SAY NO

Opinion. Coping with the crisis at science libraries: three scenarios. *The Scientist*. 4(9): 17-19; 30 April 1990.

Excerpts from three papers delivered at the February, 1990 meeting of the American Association for the Advancement of Science (AAAS) suggest reasons for and solutions to the serials problems of science libraries. Robert Peet, a professor of biology, suggests conversion from paper to compact, digital media, in order to save both money and space. A. F. Spielhaus, Jr., Executive Director of the American Geophysical Union, would like librarians and scientists to "just say no" to marginal journals. He would weight comparability factors such as price per character, impact, and length of time between submission and publication and only support the high scorers. Finally, representing the publishers' point of view, Karen Hunter of Elsevier points out the fallacy of cost comparisons, particularly between society publications and for-profit publishers. She contends that the difference is that scientists pay the cost of journals published by professional associations while librarians bear the charges for commercial publications.

SCI-TECH ONLINE

Ellen Nagle, Editor

ELEVENTH NATIONAL ONLINE MEETING

The 1990 National Online Meeting, held May 1-3, 1990 in New York City, offered 72 technical papers, product reviews, and several satellite events. Over 140 exhibits, in addition to the product reviews, provided the more than 4100 conference participants with information on the spectrum of the online industry. For the third year, the meeting included a separate CDROM Gallery with over 40 optical disc products exhibited.

Martha Williams, program chair, led off the conference with her presentation, "Highlights of the Online Database Industry and the Quality of Information and Data." After citing industry statistics she presented a "key concern . . . for the past year": quality of electronic information and data. According to Williams, "data must be well presented or packaged, appropriately documented, accurately retrieved and displayed, it must be manipulatable, and it must be analyzed and presented in a manner that is compatible with the needs of the requestor/user while at the same time being true to the sources or originators."

Williams concluded her paper with a discussion of responsibility. She described the chain of responsibility, but said that the chain does not dispense the user. "Ultimately the user must be attentive to avoid being misled or misinformed." In addition to other papers on quality assurance, the program included discussions of CD-

167

ROM technology and databases, image databases, voice recognition, software connectivity in a network environment, and the electronic reference desk.

The Fifth Integrated Online Library Systems (IOLS) Meeting was held in conjunction with the National Online Meeting. Its theme, "Converging Functions, Diverging Technologies, Growing Options" reflected the increasing demand for converging and integrating functions in library systems. Proceedings of both meetings are available from Learned Information, Inc., 143 Old Marlton Pike, Medford NJ 08555. Price for IOLS '90 is $30; $50 for the National Online Meeting. (Contributions from Thomas Mead, Dana Biomedical Library, Dartmouth-Hitchcock Medical Center are gratefully acknowledged.)

DATABASE NEWS

BRS Adds Pharmaceutical Database

The BRS collection of pharmaceutical databases has grown in size with the addition of the *IDIS Drug File*. *IDIS* is a bibliographic database with detailed indexing of articles on human drug therapy from more than 160 English-language medical and pharmaceutical journals. Each record describes the drugs, diseases and clinical concepts reported on the source article. The file's wide-ranging coverage includes information on study design, treatment efficacy, study population, dosage, administration technique, pharmacokinetics, pharmaceutics, incompatibilities, drug interactions, toxicology and side effects.

The database encompasses more than 265,000 documents from 1966 to the present. It features controlled vocabulary indexing with over 6,500 specific drug terms, over 2,400 disease condition terms, and over 100 descriptors. IDIS records include drug names based on the *United States Adopted Names* and accompanying drug numbers adopted from the American Hospital Formulary Service. Disease terms are taken from the *International Classification of Diseases*. The database also provides descriptive concept terms from the Iowa Drug Information Service thesaurus.

Charges for searching *IDIS* are $52 per connect hour. Printing of the record online is free, except for the source and microfilm file number which cost $.35 per record. The offline print charge is $.45 for any part of the record.

Fine Chemicals Database Online

DIALOG has announced an exclusive file, *Fine Chemicals Database*, produced by Chemron Incorporated. The database contains current product information for chemical manufacturing and distribution companies in North America and Europe. The focus of this new database is on sources for laboratory, specialty, and unusual chemicals used in scientific research and new product development. Fine chemicals are relatively pure chemicals typically produced in small quantities. Examples are those chemicals used in the manufacture of pharmaceuticals, biological products, perfumes, and photographic chemicals and reagents.

The file provides information on approximately 207,000 chemical products available from over 50 chemical manufacturers or distributors. Data contained in *Fine Chemicals Database* are derived from product information supplied by individual organization, catalogs, and mail questionnaires. All the information needed to purchase a chemical is supplied in each record, including catalog number, product name, address, telephone, and telefax/TWX/telex numbers. Chemical synonyms and trade names are also available for many products.

The database (File 360) can be searched by product or supplier. Products can be searched by product name, synonyms, molecular formula, CAS Registry Number, and catalog number. Segmentation of chemical substance names is available to provide access to chemically significant segments embedded within a term. Supplier information includes supplier name and company supplier code. Other searchable company information includes the city, state, and country in which the supplier is located, the telephone number, and the zip or postal code. Search results may be printed as tabular reports, with a price per data element of $.25.

Fine Chemicals Database covers the current year and is updated semiannually. The price per connect minute is $1.50. The price per full record printed online or offline is $.70.

Life Science Subfile Added

A new subfile on the Human Genome Project has been added to *Life Science Collection*, DIALOG File 76. The subfile consists of the latest in a series of abstracting journals produced by Cambridge Scientific Abstracts, *Human Genome Abstracts: Basic Research and Clinical Applications*. The Human Genome Project is a genetic research project currently underway at the National Institutes of Health in Bethesda, Maryland. Focusing on the published literature that is emerging from this international scientific study, *Human Genome Abstracts* offers a single comprehensive source of crucial new genetic discoveries. More than 2,000 sources, including proceedings of conferences. books. monographs, and databases, are reviewed to generate the citations and abstracts in this publication.

CRISP Available on BRS

The *CRISP (Computer Retrieval of Information on Scientific Products)* database is now offered by BRS. *CRISP* is a major scientific information system containing data on the research projects supported by the U.S. Public Health Service, the world's largest single organization supporting biomedical research. The majority of research included in the file falls within the broad categories of extramural programs (grants, research contracts, and cooperative agreements), as well as intramural projects conducted primarily by non-federal institutions and funded by the National Institutes of Health and the Alcohol, Drug Abuse and Mental Health Administration.

The *CRISP* database offers information on new direction, methodologies and techniques in the field of biomedicine before they appear in the published literature. The database is arranged as a series of fiscal year files, with a single fiscal year containing all research projects active during that year. Each file contains two major categories of projects: new (first-time) awards made during the fiscal year, and continuing awards, i.e., projects in at least their second year of funding. Some projects may be in progress for ten or more years.

The database covers Fiscal Year 1985 to the present, and contains 60,000 records. The cost for searching *CRISP* is $40 per connect hour. Online printing is free, except for the abstract which costs $.15 and $.20 per record.

DRUGINFO Thesaurus Updated

The second edition of the *Thesaurus for the DRUGINFO Database* is now available from the Drug Information Service, producer of *DRUGINFO* and *Alcohol Use and Abuse*. To order, send $20 plus $2 postage and handling to: Drug Information Services, University of Minnesota, 3-160 HSU-F, 308 Harvard St., S.E., Minneapolis, MN 55455. Telephone: (612) 624-6492.

EDUCATION

New Training Policies for Maxwell Online

With the consolidation of BRS and ORBIT training functions, now headquartered in McLean, Virginia, Maxwell Online has announced new training policies for both search services. According to Maxwell, these policies have been implemented to achieve a more uniform approach toward system education and awareness for all Maxwell Online Customers. New training courses and programs will be developed. Training schedules will be announced at a minimum of four-month intervals to facilitate easier registration and planning.

Prices for classes are as follows: $125 for full-day courses; $75 for half-day courses. All class participants receive four hours of online practice time with a training password, to be used within thirty days of the course date. Host sites are entitled to two free participants in each session held at the site, or, eight hours of online practice time. If you are interested in hosting training, contact the Training and Documentation Department at (703) 442-0900.

Beilstein Briefing

DIALOG has announced this new seminar for *Beilstein Online* (File 390), the online version of the *Beilstein Handbook of Organic Chemistry*. *Beilstein* is recognized by chemists as the single most complete, systematic collection of evaluated data on organic compounds. In this free two and one-half hour seminar, searchers get an overview of the database, and learn how to search and display physical properties, chemical reaction and preparation data, and molecular structures through graphic and text input.

Enrollment is limited to DIALOG users who have completed an introductory training program on DIALOG commands and search techniques. Pre-registration is required for training sessions, which may be offered for a limited time only. Phone DIALOG Training Registration at (800) 334-2564.